record pioneers

richard strauss

hans pfitzner

oskar fried

oswald kabasta

karl muck

franz von hoesslin

karl elmendorff

discographies
compiled by
john hunt

Record Pioneers

John Hunt

© John Hunt 2017

ISBN 978-1-901395-33-4

Travis & Emery Music Bookshop
17 Cecil Court
London
WC2N 4EZ
United Kingdom.
Tel. (+44) (0) 20 7240 2129.
newpublications@travis-and-emery.com

Contents

Introduction/*page 5*
Bibliography/*page 8*
Richard Strauss chronological discography/*page 9*
Richard Strauss composer discography/*page 49*
Hans Pfitzner chronological discography/*page 57*
Hans Pfitzner composer discography/*page 81*
Oskar Fried chronological discography/*page 89*
Oskar Fried composer discography/*page 111*
Oswald Kabasta chronological discography/*page 121*
Oswald Kabasta composer discography/*page 133*
Karl Muck chronological discography/*page 139*
Karl Muck composer discography/*page 147*
Franz von Hoesslin chronological discography/*page 151*
Franz von Hoesslin composer discography/*page 159*
Karl Elmendorff chronological discography/*page 161*
Karl Elmendorff composer discography/*page 185*

Record pioneers: an introduction

This discography aims at documenting the recording work of musical practitioners who were at the heart of what we might call the "shellac" era. This was the important period from the outset of orchestral recording until just before the arrival of the long-playing disc in the early 1950s.

Two of them, Richard Strauss (1864-1949) and Hans Pfitzner (1869-1949), happened to be among Germany's most prominent composers. Strauss, in particular, committed to disc a significant range of his own works; both composers also made records on which they accompanied at the piano prominent German singers of the time in *Lieder* of their own composition.

Oskar Fried (1871-1941) made the first recording of a complete Mahler symphony (No 2) only fourteen years after its composer's death – indeed he was a protégé of Gustav Mahler and himself in turn became the mentor to another Mahler specialist, Otto Klemperer. Oswald Kabasta (1896-1946), on the other hand, came to be known as something of a Bruckner specialist, having trained under the likes of Ferdinand Löwe and Franz Schmidt. Both Fried and Kabasta, however, had wider-reaching repertoire extending to French and Russian pieces. As a Jewish refugee Fried ended his working life in the USSR, whilst Kabasta ended his comparatively short recording career by committing suicide in unexplained circumstances at the end of the Second War.

introduction/continued

For the remaining three conductors in our gallery we must turn to Wagner. Karl Muck (1859-1940) was a favourite of Cosima Wagner and the first to record extensive extracts from *Parsifal*, performing that same work repeatedly at Bayreuth – until, that is, he resigned in protest at the appointment of the "foreign" conductor Arturo Toscanini. Karl Elmendorff (1891-1962) was the first to record near complete versions of both *Tannhäuser* and *Tristan und Isolde* and remained a trusted colleague at Bayreuth throughout the period of the Third Reich, leading to accusations after the War that he had been a collaborator. He also took over in Dresden when Karl Böhm departed for Vienna in 1943, and there made a number of significant operatic recordings for the *Reichsrundfunk* of repertoire beyond Wagner. Elmendorff can best be described as the epitomy of the German *Kapellmeister* in the best sense of that word, contributing positively to the tradition exemplified by Böhm himself, not to mention by Wilhelm Furtwängler, Hans Knappertsbusch, Herbert von Karajan and, after a gap of two decades, by Christian Thielemann.

In contrast to Elmendorff, Franz von Hoesslin (1885-1946) was an outspoken opponent of the Nazi regime. Refusing to divorce his Jewish wife, he was nonetheless permitted to continue

introduction/concluded

working at Bayreuth until 1942 because of his favoured position with Winifred Wagner. Over a decade earlier Hoesslin had made the very first gramophonic attempts to set down a potted *Ring* cycle for the French Pathe company, using lesser known singers and a Paris-based orchestra.

The discographies follow the pattern of other recent ones, listing recording sessions in chronological sequence but with a composer listing added for cross-reference. Each session is headed with details of record company, with dates and venue where known. Then follow names of participating orchestras and soloists. A left-hand column lists 78rpm matrix numbers, which often – but not always – give an indication of the order in which musical sections were recorded. To the right of each pair of matrix numbers appear the shellac catalogue numbers for the main territories of issue. Finally at the bottom come details of any major LP and CD reissues.

Colleagues who helped with information are gratefully acknowledged: John Baker, Roderick Krüsemann, Alan Newcombe and Neville Sumpter.

<u>John Hunt</u>   2016

8
Bibliography

The following reference works proved to be invaluable in compiling these discograpies :-

Richard Strauss: Chronik zu Leben und Werk
Franz und Florian Trenner 2003

Richard Strauss's Recordings: Composer discography
Peter Morse 1974

Beiträge zum Oswald Kabasta-Symposion
Engelbert M. Exl und Michael Nagy 1995

World's Encyclopaedia of Recorded Music
F.F. Clough and G.J. Cuming 1952-1955

Great Wagner Conductors: A Listener's Companion
Jonathan Brown 2012

Sächsische Staatskapelle Dresden: A discography
John Hunt 2002

Wagner im Festspielhaus: A Bayreuth discography
John Hunt 2006

plus
Electrola, Columbia and Grammophon catalogues covering the period 1930-1950

RICHARD STRAUSS: CHRONOLOGICAL DISCOGRAPHY

001/16 february 1906/recordings in leipzig for the welte-mignon re-producing piano roll

richard strauss, piano

roll no. 1182/strauss fragments from salome
lp: welte 673/joker SM 1182
cd: tacet 137

roll no. 1183/strauss tanz der sieben schleier/salome
lp: welte 673/columbia (usa) ML 4295/joker SM 1182/ telefunken TM 97009/GMA 65/HT 18/WE 28003/SL 25057
cd: tacet 137/naxos 8.110678

roll no. 1184/strauss liebesszene/ein heldenleben
lp: welte 673/columbia (usa) ML 4295/joker SM 1182/ telefunken TM 97009/GMA 65/HT 18/WE 28003/SL 25057
cd: tacet 137

roll no. 1185/strauss liebesszene/feuersnot
lp: welte 673/joker SM 1182/telefunken WE 28004/SL 25057
cd: tacet 137/documents 232 597

roll no. 1186/strauss auf stillem waldespfad/stimmungsbilder
this recording remains unpublished

roll no. 1187/strauss an einsamer quelle/stimmungsbilder
lp: welte 673/joker SM 1182
cd: tacet 137

001/1906/welte-mignon piano rolls/concluded

roll no. 1188/strauss intermezzo/stimmungsbilder
lp: welte 673/joker SM 1182/columbia (usa) ML 4295
cd: tacet 137/documents 232 597

roll no. 1189/strauss träumerei am kamin/stimmungsbilder
lp: welte 673/joker SM 1182/asco A-119/telefunken
WE 28004/HT 38/GMA 91/SLA 25057
cd: tacet 137/documents 232 597

roll no. 1190/strauss heidebild/stimmungsbilder
this recording remains unpublished

roll no. 1191/strauss heimliche aufforderung
lp: columbia (usa) ML 4295
cd: tacet 137
the piano roll remained unpublished

roll no. unknown/strauss cäcilie
cd: tacet 137

002/13 april 1916/recordings in leipzig for hupfeld animatic piano roll

richard strauss, piano

roll no. 54852/strauss minuet/ariadne auf naxos

roll no. 54853/strauss music from act two/ariadne auf naxos

rolls nos. 54854-58456/strauss music from eine alpensinfonie

roll no. 54857/strauss liebesszene/ein heldenleben

roll no. 54858/strauss music from josephslegende

these rolls have not been re-issued in any other format

003/5, 6, 13, 15 and 20 december 1916/grammophon acoustic sessions in berlin

staatskapelle berlin/richard strauss

strauss der burger als edelmann, 1912 suite from the incidental music (including the overture/ariadne auf naxos)

1047 LC	69522/65853
1054 ½ LC	
1048 ½ LC	69523/65854
1051 ½ LC	
1049 LC	69524/65855
1050 LC	
1053 ½ LC	69658/66289

lp: rococo 2015 (69658 only)
cd: crq editions CRQCD 155-157

003/december 1916/grammophon sessions/concluded

strauss don juan op 20

1057 LC	69525/65856
1058 LC	
1059 LC	69526/65857
1060 LC	

cd: crq editions CRQCD 155-157

assistant conductor george szell recalled having led the first session for don juan, but there is no evidence to support the claim that he recorded the entire work in place of richard strauss

strauss till eulenspiegels lustige streiche op 28

1061	69527/65858
1062 ½	
1063	69528/65859
1064 LC	

cd: crq editions CRQCD 155-157

strauss der rosenkavalier: waltz sequence arranged by otto singer

1065 LC	69529/65860
1066 LC	

cd: crq editions CRQCD 155-157

004/november-december 1919/grammophon acoustic sessions in berlin

richard strauss, piano/robert hutt, tenor

strauss lieder: breit über mein haupt; morgen
19248 ½ L   62363
19249 L
lp: rococo 5017
cd: symposium 1225/documents 232 597
also issued on lp and cd by preiser

richard strauss, piano/heinrich schlusnus, baritone

strauss lieder: heimkehr; ich liebe dich
14102r   62364
14103r
lp: rococo 5017
cd: symposium 1225/documents 232 597
also issued on lp and cd by preiser

004/1919/grammophon sessions in berlin/concluded

richard strauss, piano/heinrich schlusnus, baritone

strauss lieder: ruhe meine seele; zueignung; die nacht; das geheimnis

14106r	62365
14120r	
14121r	62366
14125r	

lp: rococo 5017
cd: symposium 1225/documents 232 597/deutsche grammophon 479 2703
also issued on lp and cd by preiser

005/30-31 december 1921/brunswick acoustic sessions in new york

brunswick studio orchestra/richard strauss

strauss tanz der sieben schleier/salome; menuett und intermezzo/der bürger als edelmann

7001	50002
7004	
7005	50017
7007	

cd: crq editions CRQCD 155-157

006/30-31 december 1921/recordings in new york for ampico piano rolls

richard strauss, piano

roll no. 1291/strauss zueignung

roll no. 60251/an einsamer quelle/stimmungsbilder

roll no. 60301/strauss zueignung/accompaniment for contralto version

roll no. 60351/strauss zueignung/accompaniment for soprano version

roll no. 60431/strauss allerseelen/accompaniment for baritone version

roll no. 60441/strauss allerseelen/accompaniment for soprano version

roll no. 60561/strauss traum durch die dämmerung/ accompaniment for baritone version

roll no. 60571/strauss traum durch die dämmerung/ accompaniment for soprano version

these rolls have not been re-issued in any format

007/18-19 january 1922/columbia acoustic sessions in london petty france studios

london symphony orchestra/richard strauss

strauss don juan op 20
75034 L 1419
75035
75036 L 1420
75037
cd: crq editions CRQCD 155-157
this version of don juan has an 11-bar cut in order to accommodate it on the two ten-inch discs

strauss der rosenkavalier: waltz sequence arranged by otto singer
75038 L 1421
75039
cd: crq editions CRQCD 155-157

strauss tanz der sieben schleier/salome
75040 L 1422
75041
cd: crq editions CRQCD 155-157

strauss

008/24-26 february 1926/grammophon sessions in berlin markgrafenstrasse studios using the pallophotophone (light-ray) system

staatskapelle berlin/richard strauss

beethoven symphony no 7 in a op 92
339 ½ bg	69836/brunswick 25010
340bg	
341bg	69837/brunswick 25011
342bg	
343bg	69838/brunswick 25012
344bg	
345bg	69839/brunswick 25013
346bg	

lp: thomas clear TCL 2584
cd: koch 3-7115-2/dante LYS 216/documents 232 597/ naxos 8.110926/deutsche grammophon 479 2703
first movement of the symphony was cut in order to fit the complete work on eight shellac sides

mozart symphony no 39 in e flat K543
347bg	69833
348bg	
349bg	69834
350bg	
351bg	69835
352bg	

lp: heliodor 88 022
cd: koch 3-7076-2/documents 232 597/deutsche grammophon 479 2703

009/4-5 march 1926/grammophon sessions in berlin markgrafenstrasse studios using the pallophotophone (light-ray) system

staatskapelle berlin/richard strauss

strauss ein heldenleben op 40
360bg	69840/brunswick 25000
361bg	
362bg	69841/brunswick 25001
363bg	
364bg	69842/brunswick 25002
6bm	
366bg	69843/brunswick 25003
367bg	
368bg	69844/brunswick 25004
369bg	

cd: crq editions CRQCD 155-157

010/13-14 april 1926/hmv sessions in london queens hall

augmented london tivoli theatre orchestra/richard strauss

strauss der rosenkavalier: orchestral transcription to accompany the 1925 silent film, with added march

CR 280 II   D 1094/W 916/EJ 35/victor 9281
CR 281 I
CR 283 I   D 1095/W 917/EJ 36/victor 9282
CR 284 IA
CR 285 I   D 1096/W 915/EJ 37/victor 9280
CR 286 IA
CR 282 I   D 1097/W 918/EJ 38/victor 9283
cd: emi 754 6102/dutton CDBP 9785

011/1-2 november 1926/grammophon sessions in berlin using the pallophotophone (light-ray) system

staatskapelle berlin/richard strauss

mozart symphony no 41 in c K551 "jupiter"
180bm	69845/brunswick 25017
181bm	
182bm	69846/brunswick 25018
183bm	
184bm	69847/brunswick 25019
185bm	
186bm	69848/brunswick 25020

cd: koch 3-7076-2/deutsche grammophon 431 8742/479 2703

strauss tod und verklärung op 24
219bm	69849/brunswick 25026
220bm	
221bm	69850/brunswick 25027
222bm	
223bm	69851/brunswick 25028
224bm	

lp: heliodor 2548 748/deutsche grammophon 2740 160
cd: deutsche grammophon 429 9252/479 2703

strauss

011/1926/grammophon sessions in berlin/concluded
strauss intermezzo: interlude and waltz scene
225bm   69852/brunswick 25014
226bm
229bm   69853/brunswick 25015/engl.brunswick 80027
230bm
lp: deutsche grammophon 2548 748 (interlude)/
acanta 72.22179-2 (waltz)
cd: documents 232 597 (interlude)/crq editions CRQCD 155-157
acanta edition incorrectly describes orchestra as dresden staatskapelle

strauss der rosenkavalier: waltz sequence arranged by otto singer
227bm   69854/brunswick 25016/engl. brunswick 80009
228bm
cd: documents 232 597/crq editions CRQCD 155-157

012/28 march 1927/grammophon sessions in berlin hochschule für musik

staatskapelle berlin/richard strauss

mozart symphony no 40 in g minor K550
250bi   69864
251bi
252bi   69865
253bi
254bi   69866
255bi
lp: thomas clear TCL 2584
cd: koch 3-7076-2/deutsche grammophon 479 2703/ documents 232 597

013/2 april 1927/grammophon sessions in berlin hochschule für musik

staatskapelle berlin/richard strauss

strauss intermezzo: interlude and waltz scene
261bi   69867
262bi
263bi   69868
264bi
lp: rococo 2015 (interlude)/deutsche grammophon 2740 160 (interlude)
cd: deutsche grammophon 429 9252/479 2703 (interlude)/ crq editions CRQCD 155-157

strauss der rosenkavalier: waltz sequence arranged by otto singer
265bi   69863
266bi
lp: deutsche grammophon 2740 160
cd: deutsche grammophon 429 9252/479 2703/ dante LYS 393/crq editions CRQCD 155-157

014/25 november 1927/grammophon sessions in berlin markgrafenstrasse studios

staatskapelle berlin/richard strauss

mozart symphony no 40 in g minor K550
296be   69869/95442/brunswick 90082
297be
298be   69870/95443/brunswick 90083
299be
300be   69871/95444/brunswick 90084
301be
302be   69872/95445/brunswick 90085
lp: deutsche grammophon 642 010/2721 070/heliodor 88 002
cd: koch 3-7119-2/deutsche grammophon 431 8742

015/1 october 1928/grammophon sessions in berlin

staatskapelle berlin/richard strauss

beethoven symphony no 5 in c minor op 67

1383bm I	66814/brunswick 90172/fonit 96057/91014
1384bm I	
1385bm I	66815/brunswick 90173/fonit 96058/91015
1386bm I	
1402bm I	66816/brunswick 90174/fonit 96059/91016
1403bm I	
1404bm I	66817/brunswick 90175/fonit 96060/91017
1405bm I	

lp: rococo 2015
cd: dante LYS 216/koch 3-7113-2/naxos 8.110926/
dutton CDBP 9813/documents 232 597/
deutsche grammophon 479 2703

mozart die zauberflöte overture K620

1406bm I	66826/brunswick 90255/decca CA 8106
1407bm I	

lp: deutsche grammophon 2548 736
cd: koch 3-7119-2/deutsche grammophon 439 8742/479 2703/
dutton CDBP 9785/documents 232 597
matrix numbers 1406bm i-1407bm I were replaced in 1939
by 1239gs-1240gs

016/6, 10 and 17 december 1928/grammophon sessions in berlin hochschule für musik

philharmonisches orchester berlin/richard strauss

cornelius der barbier von bagdad overture
1496bm I   66936
1497bm I
lp: deutsche grammophon 2548 736
cd: koch 3-7119-2/documents 232 597/dutton CDBP 9785/ deutsche grammophon 479 2703

weber euryanthe overture
1497 ½ b ml   66828
1498bm I
lp: deutsche grammophon 2548 736
cd: koch 3-7119-2/documents 232 597/dutton CDBP 9785/ deutsche grammophon 479 2703

gluck iphigenia in aulis overture, arranged by wagner
1500bm I   66829/brunswick 90110/french polydor 516625
1501bm I
lp: deutsche grammophon 2548 736/2740 259
cd: koch 3-7119-2/documents 232 597/dutton CDBP 9785/ deutsche grammophon 479 2703

016/december 1928/grammophon sessions/concluded
wagner der fliegende holländer overture
1506bm I   66830/brunswick 90120
1507bm I
lp: deutsche grammophon 2548 736/2721 113
cd: koch 3-7119-2/documents 232 597/dutton CDBP 9785/ deutsche grammophon 479 2703

wagner lohengrin prelude
1508bm I   unpublished
1509bm I

wagner tristan und isolde prelude/*with concert ending*
1510bm I   66832
1511bm I
lp: deutsche grammophon 2548 736
cd: koch 3-7119-2/documents 232 597/dutton CDBP 9785/ deutsche grammophon 479 2703

strauss salome: tanz der sieben schleier
1520 ½ bm I   66827/brunswick 90088/decca CA 8017/fonit 91020
1521bm I
45: deutsche grammophon EPL 30538
lp: rococo 2015/first editions FER 1/deutsche grammophon 2548 722/2740 160/2740 259
cd: koch 3-7119-2/deutsche grammophon 479 2703
rococo edition incorrectly described orchestra as staatskapelle berlin

**017/5 june 1929/grammophon sessions in berlin
hochschule für musik**

staatskapelle berlin/richard strauss

strauss till eulenspiegels lustige streiche op 28
779 ½ bi I   66887/brunswick 90044/french polydor 51633
780 ½ bi I
781bi I   66888/brunswick 90045/french polydor 51634
782bi I
45: deutsche grammophon EPL 30431
lp: first editions FER 1/deutsche grammophon 2548 722/2740 136
cd: deutsche grammophon 429 9252/479 2703
*matrix numbers 779 ½ bi I-782 bi were replaced in 1939 by
1244gs ID-1247gs ID; EPL 30431 was incorrectly dated 1939*

strauss don juan op 20
791bi I   66902/brunswick 90046/decca CA 8126/fonit 91083
792bi I
793bi I   66903/brunswick 90047/decca CA 8127/fonit 91084
794bi I
lp: deutsche grammophon 2548 748/2721 070/2740 160
cd: deutsche grammophon 429 9252/479 2703/
dutton CDBP 9720/documents 232 597
*matrix numbers 791bi I-794bi I were replaced in 1939 by
1248gs ID-1251gs ID; 2721 070 was incorrectly dated 1932;
original discs were also published in automatic coupling with
the numbers 67355ac-67356ac*

018/23 and 28 june 1930/grammophon sessions in berlin lützowstrasse studios

staatskapelle berlin/richard strauss
josef wolfsthal, viola/enrico mainardi, cello

strauss der burger als edelmann: suite from the incidental music

408bs II	95392/brunswick 90130
409 ½ bs II	
410bs II	95393/brunswick 90131
414bs II	
415bs II	95394/brunswick 90132
416bs II	
417bs II	95395/brunswick 90133
418 bs II	
419bs II	95396/brunswick 90134

lp: decca (usa) DL 9576/deutsche grammophon 2740 160
cd: deutsche grammophon 429 9252/479 2703/dutton CDBP 9746

019/1 may 1932/radio recording in berlin

berliner funkorchester/richard strauss

strauss don juan op 20
lp: acanta DE 23055
cd: dante LYS 394
the surviving recording also includes a short rehearsal extract

020/october 1933/grammophon sessions in berlin

staatskapelle berlin/richard strauss
enrico mainardi, cello/karl reitz, viola/georg kniestädt, violin

strauss don quixote op 35

724 be I	27320/95485/35007/brunswick 90319/decca LY 6087
725 ½ be i	
726be I	27321/95486/35008/brunswick 90320/decca LY 6088
727be I	
728be I	27322/95487/35009/brunswick 90321/decca LY 6089
729 ½ be I	
730be I	27323/95488/35010/brunswick 90322/decca LY 6090
731be I	
732 ½ be I	27324/95489/35011/brunswick 90323/decca LY 6091

lp: deutsche grammophon 2740 160
cd: deutsche grammophon 429 9252/479 2703/
dutton CDBP 9746/documents 232 597

021/15 november 1933/concert recording in berlin philharmonie at the inauguration ceremony of the reichsmusikkammer

philharmonisches orchester berlin/richard strauss

strauss festliches präludium op 61
reichsrundfunkgesellschaft matrix numbers 1509-1511
this recording remains unpublished

022/29-30 june 1936/experimental recordings in munich senderrraum des reichsenders

orchester des reichsenders münchen/richard strauss

strauss eine alpensinfonie op 64
cd: music and arts CD 1057

strauss don juan op 20
reichsrundfunk matrix numbers 31550-31554
cd: music and arts CD 1057

023/1 august 1936/film and sound recordings in berlin olympistadion at opening ceremony of the olympic games

philharmonisches orchester berlin/bruno-kittel-chor/richard strauss

strauss olympische hymne
dvd: c major entertainment 729 908
this is a more extensive excerpt from the film than that shown in leni riefenstahl's film "triumph des willens"

024/7 november 1936/bbc concert recordings in london queens hall

sächsische staatskapelle dresden/richard strauss
karl hesse, cello/georg seifert, viola

strauss don quixote op 35
cd: appian recordings APR 5527

strauss till eulenspiegels lustige streiche op 28
only from beginning up to figure 24 bar 4
cd: appian recordings APR 5527

025/15 december 1936/reichsrundfunk concert recording in berlin saal 1 des deutschlandsenders

orchester des deutschlandsenders berlin/richard strauss

strauss macbeth op 23
reichsrundfunk matrix numbers 33790-33794
cd: music and arts CD 1057/appian recordings APR 5527

strauss

026/23 february 1937/reichsrundfunk recording in munich senderraum des deutschlandsenders

orchester des reichsenders münchen/richard strauss

strauss tod und verklärung op 24
reichsrundfunk matrix numbers 34723-34729
cd: music and arts CD 1057

027/1939/reichsrundfunk recordings in berlin

orchester des reichsenders berlin/richard strauss

also sprach zarathustra op 30
lp: acanta DE 23055
cd: documents 232 597

till eulenspiegels lustige streiche op 28
lp: acanta DE 23055
cd: dante LYS 393/documents 232 597

**028/12 november 1940/grammophon sessions in munich
kongressaal des deutschen museums**

bayerisches staatsorchester/richard strauss

japanische festmusik op 84
1086 ¾ ge 5   67599/Japanese polydor 35001
1087ge 5
1088 ¾ ge 5   67600/Japanese polydor 35002
1089 ge 5
lp: first editions FER 1/deutsche grammophon
2548 722/2740 160
cd: preiser 90205/documents 232 597/
deutsche grammophon 479 2703

**029/7-9 may 1941/electrola sessions in munich
kongressaal des deutschen museums**

bayerisches staatsorchester/richard strauss

strauss eine alpensinfonie op 64
2RA 5035	DB 5662
2RA 5036	
2RA 5037	DB 5663
2RA 5038	
2RA 5039	DB 5664
2RA 5040	
2RA 5041	DB 5665
2RA 5042	
2RA 5043	DB 5666
2RA 5044	
2RA 5045	DB 5667

lp: E 80824/hmv COLH 311/seraphim (usa) 60006
cd: preiser 90205/dutton CDBP 9720/emi 754 6102/ documents 232 597

030/3-5 june 1941/sound sessions in munich for a projected film by tobis-filmgesellschaft (planned with landscape and nature shots)

bayerisches staatsorchester/richard strauss

strauss eine alpensinfonie op 64
the recording remains unpublished

031/22-24 august 1941/grammophon sessions in munich kongressaal des deutschen museums

bayerisches staatsorchester/richard strauss

strauss ein heldenleben op 40
1560 ½ ge 5   67756/fonit 96096
1561 ½ ge 5
1562 ½ ge 5   67757/fonit 96097
1563 ½ ge 5
1564 5/8 ge 5   67758/fonit 96098
1565 ½ ge 5
1566ge 5   67759/fonit 96099
1567 ½ ge 5
1568 ½ ge 5   67760/fonit 96100
1569 ½ ge 5
lp: decca (usa) DL 9602/deutsche grammophon 2548 713/2740 160
cd: preiser 90205/documents 232 597/ deutsche grammophon 479 2703

original edition was also published twice in automatic coupling with the numbers 67761-67765 and 69427-69431; 2548 713 was incorrectly dated 1926

031/august 1941/grammophon sessions in munich/concluded

strauss don quixote op 35

oswald uhl, cello/philipp haass, viola/placidus morasch, violin

1570 ½ ge 5	67800
1571ge 5	
1572 ½ ge 5	67801
1573 ½ ge 5	
1574	67802
1576 ½ ge 5	
1577 ½ ge 5	67803
1578ge 5	
1579 ½ ge 5	67804

lp: decca (usa) DL 9539

cd: preiser 90205/dante LYS 394/dutton CDBP 9813/ deutsche grammophon 479 2703

original edition also published in automatic coupling with the numbers 69432-69436

strauss der rosenkavalier: waltz sequence arranged by richard strauss

1580 5/8 ge 5	67729/fonit 96077
1581 ½ ge 5	

45: deutsche grammophon EPL 30538

lp: first editions FER 1/deutsche grammophon 2548 722/2740 160

cd: preiser 90205/documents 232 597/dutton CDBP 9720/ CDBP 9785/deutsche grammophon 479 2703

032/august 1941/experimental telefunken sessions in munich for long-playing disc (5 single-sided discs planned, each of approximately 7 minutes duration)

bayerisches staatsorchester/richard strauss

strauss ein heldenleben op 40
this recording remains unpublished

033/3 december 1941/stage recording in vienna staatsoper

chor und orchester der wiener staatsoper/richard strauss
esther rethy/else böttcher/anny konetzni/jakob sabel/
erich kunz/marjan rus/herbert alsen

mozart idomeneo, in the adaptation by richard strauss and lothar wallerstein
cd: koch 3-1453-2
fragmentary recording only, totalling approximately 19 minutes in duration

034/15 february 1942/stage recording in vienna staatsoper

orchester der wiener staatsoper/richard strauss
else schulz/else schürhoff/paul schöffler/anton dermota/
dora with/Josef witt/hermann gallos/william wernigk/
willy franter/anton arnold/erich kunz/herbert alsen/
hans schweiger/carl bissuti/karl ettl

strauss salome
cd: koch 3-1453-2
*fragmentary recording only, totalling approximately
25 minutes in duration*

035/12 march 1942/reichsrundfunk recording in vienna musikvereinssaal

wiener philharmoniker/richard strauss

strauss till eulenspiegels lustige streiche op 28
cd: music and arts CD 1057
reichsrundfunk matrix numbers 68219-68222

036/29 march 1942/reichsrundfunk recording in vienna musikvereinssaal

wiener philharmoniker/richard strauss

strauss also sprach zarathustra op 30
cd: music and arts CD 1057
reichsrundfunk matrix numbers 68359-68367

037/6 may 1942/stage recording in vienna staatsoper

orchester der wiener staatsoper/richard strauss
else schulz/mela bugarinovic/hans hotter/anton dermota/
Joachim sattler

strauss salome
cd: koch 3-1453-2
fragmentary recording only, totalling approximately
14 minutes in duration

038/1942-1943/reichsrundfunk recordings in vienna funkhaus

richard strauss, piano/anton dermota, tenor

strauss lieder: heimliche aufforderung; die nacht; zueignung; ich liebe dich; seitdem dein aug; breit über mein haupt; ich trage meine minne; du meines herzens krönelein
lp: rococo 5350/preiser PR 3262
cd: preiser 93262/documents 232 597

strauss lieder: heimkehr; seitdem dein aug; all mein gedanken; glückes genug; in goldener fülle; sehnsucht
lp: preiser PR 3261
cd: preiser 93261/documents 232 597

41   *strauss*

038/1942-1943/reichsrundfunk recordings in vienna/concluded
richard strauss, piano/maria reining, soprano

strauss lieder: meinem kinde; freundliche vision; cäcilie; traum durch die dämmerung; zueignung; waldseligkeit
lp: rococo 5350/preiser PR 3262
cd: preiser 93262/documents 232 597

richard strauss, piano/lea piltti, soprano

strauss lieder: heimkehr; ständchen; ich schwebe; kling kling!; all mein gedanken; schlagende herzen
lp: rococo 5350/preiser PR 3262
cd: preiser 93262/documents 232 597

richard strauss, piano/hilde konetzni, soprano

strauss lieder: schlechtes wetter; blick vom oberen belvedere; du meines herzens krönelein; ach lieb ich muss nun scheiden
lp: preiser PR 3261
cd: preiser 93261/documents 232 597

richard strauss, piano/alfred poell, baritone

strauss lieder: ach weh mir unglückhaftem manne; wozu noch mädchen?; das rosenband; winterliebe; ruhe meine seele; heimliche aufforderung
lp: preiser PR 3261
cd: preiser 93261/documents 232 597

039/17 february 1943/reichsrundfunk recording in vienna funkhaus

wiener philharmoniker/richard strauss

strauss sinfonia domestica op 53
lp: vox PL 7220/turnabout TV 4363/intercord INT 120.929/
eterna 826 208/clavier CT 1505/vanguard SRV 329
cd: preiser 90206/dante LYS 291/documents 232 597/
deutsche grammophon 435 3212/435 3332
many editions incorrectly dated 1944; deutsche grammophon issues also include wagner meistersinger overture attributed to strauss but actually conducted by karl böhm

040/25 august 1943/reichsrundfunk recording in munich odeon

orchester des reichssenders münchen/richard strauss
julius patzak, tenor

strauss orchesterlieder: ich trage meine minne; heimliche aufforderung; morgen; ständchen
lp: ed smith recordings EJS 463/rococo 5348/acanta 10.22055-9 (all except morgen)/22.21807-9 (ich trage meine mine)
cd: bella voce BLV 107 210/documents 232 597
ed smith edition incorrectly dated 1944

041/9-11 june 1944/ufa film recording (sound and vision) in vienna musikvereinssaal

wiener philharmoniker/richard strauss

strauss till eulenspiegels lustige streiche op 28
complete performance edited from the total of
50 minutes footage; extended extracts can be
viewed in the documentary by eric schulz
issued on dvd c major entertainment 729 908

042/12 june 1944/reichsrundfunk recordings (magnetophonkonzert) in vienna musikvereinssaal to mark the composer's eightietn birthday

wiener philharmoniker/richard strauss

strauss der burger als edelmann: suite from the incidental music
lp: urania (usa) RS 7-8/regent 5013/eterna 826 205/ clavier CT 1503/vanguard SRV 326/discocorp SID 710
cd: preiser 90216/documents 232 597

strauss don juan op 20
lp: clavier CT 1501/vanguard SRV 328/eterna 826 204/ discocorp SID 710
cd: preiser 90216

**043/13 june 1944/reichsrrundfunk recordings
(magnetophonkonzert) in vienna musikvereinssaal
marking the composer's eightieth birthday**

wiener philharmoniker/richard strauss

strauss also sprach zarathustra op 30
lp: clavier CT 1502/vanguard SRV 325/eterna 826 207/discocorp SID 710/turnabout THS 65021/olympic 8111
cd: preiser 90206

strauss tod und verklärung op 24
lp: clavier CT 1501/vanguard SRV 328/eterna 826 204/
discocorp SID 710
cd: preiser 90206/documents 232 597

**044/14 june 1944/reichsrundfunk recordings
(magnetophonkonzert) in vienna musikvereinssaal
marking the composer's eightieth birthday**

wiener philharmoniker/richard strauss

strauss tanzsuite nach francois couperin
cd: documents 232 597

strauss festliches präludium op 61
this recording remains unpublished

045/15 june 1944/reichsrundfunk recording (magnetophonkonzert) in vienna musikvereinssaal marking the composer's eightieth birthday

wiener philharmoniker/richard strauss

strauss till eulenspiegels lustige streiche op 28
lp: clavier CT 1503/vanguard SRV 326/eterna 826 326/
discocorp SID 710
cd: preiser 90206/deutsche grammophon 435 3332/435 3212

strauss ein heldenleben op 40
lp: clavier CT 1504/vanguard SRV 327/eterna 826 205/
discocorp SID 710
cd: dante LYS 393/preiser 90206

046/1944/reichsrundfunk recording in berlin

orchester des reichsenders berlin/richard strauss

strauss schlagobers-walzer
lp: clavier CT 1501/vanguard SRV 328/eterna 826 204/
discocorp SID 710/turnabout THS 65021/olympic 8111
vanguard, discocorp and olympic editions incorrectly described as wiener philharmoniker

047/11 june 1947/swiss radio concert in lugano studio radiofonico del campo marzio

orchestra della svizzera italiana/richard strauss
annette brun, soprano

strauss orchesterlieder: morgen; allerseelen; ich trage meine minne; das rosenband
cd: cpo classics 777 9902

strauss bläserserenade op 7; strauss der burger als edelmann: suite from the incidental music
these recordings remain unpublished

048/19 october 1947/restored bbc broadcast acetates from concert in london royal albert hall

philharmonia orchestra/richard strauss
alfred blumen, piano

strauss don juan op 20; burleske in d minor; sinfonia domestica op 53
cd: testament SBT2-1441
don juan and sinfonia domestica have gaps in the music due to change-over of acetates; cd also includes section of don juan before restoration treatment

049/29 october 1947/restored bbc broadcast acetates from concert in london royal albert hall

bbc symphony orchestra/richard strauss

strauss till eulenspiegels lustige streiche op 28
cd: testament SBT2-1441
gaps in the music due to change over of acetates

050/10 june 1949/film fragment in munich prinzregententheater for a planned documentary about the composer

bayerisches staatsorchester/richard strauss
georg hann, bass-baritone

strauss der rosenkavalier: final bars of act two
this has been included in countless film documentaries

051/june-july 1949/film fragment in garmisch for a planned documentary about the composer

richard strauss, piano

strauss daphne: final bars of the opera
this has been included in countless film documentaries

052/13 july 1949/bayerischer rundfunk recording in munich

münchner rundfunkorchester/richard strauss

strauss capriccio: mondscheinmusik
cd: crq editions CRQCD 155-157

RICHARD STRAUSS: COMPOSER DISCOGRAPHY
session numbers enable cross-reference to the main chronological discography

LUDWIG VAN BEETHOVEN (1770-1827)
symphony no 5 in c minor op 67
015/berlin 1928

symphony no 7 in a op 92
008/berlin 1926

PETER CORNELIUS (1824-1874)
der barbier von bagdad: overture
016/berlin 1928

CHRISTOPH WILLIBALD GLUCK (1714-1787)
iphigenia in aulis: overture arranged by wagner
016/berlin 1928

composer discography/continued

WOLFGANG AMADEUS MOZART (1756-1791)

symphony no 39 in e flat K543
008/berlin 1926

symphony no 40 in g minor K550
012/berlin 1927   014/berlin 1927

symphony no 41 in c K551 "jupiter"
011/berlin 1926

idomeneo: fragmentary excerpts
033/vienna 1941

die zauberflöte: overture
015/berlin 1928

composer discography/continued
RICHARD STRAUSS (1864-1949)
eine alpensinfonie op 64
022/munich 1936   029/munich 1941
030/munich 1941

eine alpensinfonie: piano roll excerpt
002/leipzig 1916

also sprach zarathustra op 30
027/berlin 1939   036/vienna 1942
043/vienna 1944

ariadne auf naxos: overture to the opera
003/berlin 1916

ariadne auf naxos: piano roll excerpts
002/leipzig 1916

der burger als edelmann: suite from the incidental music
003/berlin 1916   005/new york 1921
018/berlin 1930   042/vienna 1944
047/lugano 1947
each recorded version varies in content

composer discography/continued

strauss burleske in d minor
048/london 1947

capriccio: mondscheinmusik
052/munich 1949

daphne: piano transcription fragment
051/munich 1949

don juan op 20

003/berlin 1916	007/london 1922
017/berlin 1929	019/berlin 1932
022/munich 1936	042/vienna 1944
048/london 1947	

don juan: rehearsal fragment
029/berlin 1932

don quixote op 35

020/berlin 1933	024/london 1936
031/munich 1941	

festliches präludium op 61

021/berlin 1933	044/vienna 1944

composer discography/continued

strauss feuersnot: liebesszene piano roll
001/leipzig 1906

ein heldenleben op 40
009/berlin 1926   032/munich 1941
045/vienna 1944

ein heldenleben: piano roll excerpt
001/leipzig 1906   002/leipzig 1916

intermezzo: interlude and waltz scene
011/berlin 1926   013/berlin 1927

japanische festmusik op 84
028/munich 1940

josephslegende: piano roll excerpt
002/leipzig 1916

lieder with piano accompaniment
004/berlin 1919   038/vienna 1942

lieder: piano accompaniment piano rolls
001/leipzig 1906   006/new york 1921

macbeth op 23
025/berlin 1936

composer discography/continued

strauss olympische hymne
023/berlin 1936

orchesterlieder
040/munich 1943   047/lugano 1947

der rosenkavalier: act two finale
050/munich 1949

der rosenkavalier: waltzes arranged by singer
003/berlin 1916   007/london 1922
011/berlin 1926   013/berlin 1927

der rosenkavalier: waltzes arranged by strauss
031/munich 1941

der rosenkavalier: suite for the silent film
010/london 1926

salome: fragments from the opera
034/vienna 1942   037/vienna 1942

composer discography/continued

strauss salome: piano roll excerpts
001/leipzig 1906

salome: tanz der sieben schleier
005/new york 1921   007/london 1922
016/berlin 1928

schlagobers waltz
046/berlin 1944

serenade für bläser op 7
047/lugano 1947

sinfonia domestica op 53
039/vienna 1943   048/london 1947

stimmungsbilder für klavier op 9: piano roll excerpts
001/leipzig 1906

tanzsuite nach couperin
044/vienna 1944

till eulenspiegels lustige streiche op 28
003/berlin 1916   017/berlin 1929
024/london 1936

tod und verklärung op 24
011/berlin 1926   026/munich 1937
043/vienna 1944

composer discography/concluded

RICHARD WAGNER (1813-1833)
der fliegende holländer overture
016/berlin 1928

lohengrin prelude
016/berlin 1928

tristan und isolde: prelude with the concert ending
016/berlin 1928

CARL MARIA VON WEBER (1786-1826)
euryanthe overture
016/berlin 1928

HANS PFITZNER: CHRONOLOGICAL DISCOGRAPHY

001/1923/grammophon acoustic sessions in berlin

philharmonisches orchester berlin/hans pfitzner
orchestra described for these sessions as neues sinfonieorchester berlin

pfitzner die rose vom liebesgarten: trauermarsch
221az   65909/69628
222az
pfitzner das käthchen von heilbronn: epilogue and march
223az   65910/69629
224az
pfitzner das christelflein overture
225az   65869/69649
226az
beethoven symphony no 7: abridged versions of second and fourth movements
227az   66285/69648
228az
weber der freischütz overture
229az   65911/69620
230az
231az   65912/69621

001/1923/grammophon sessions in berlin/concluded

schumann symphony no 4 in d minor op 120

1406az	66282/69625
1407az	
1408az	66283/69626
234az	
232az	66284/69627
233az	

beethoven symphony no 6 in f op 68 "pastoral"

239az	66254/69642
240az	
241az	66255/69643
235az	
236az	66256/69644
237az	
238az	66257/69645
1412az	
1413az	66258/69646
1414az	
1415az	66259/69647

beethoven symphony no 8 in f op 93: second movement

1405 ½ az	66259/69647

pfitzner das fest auf solhaug: overture and act two finale

65949

65950

002/1924/grammophon acoustic session in berlin

philharmonisches orchester berlin/hans pfitzner

weber preciosa overture
1527as   65948
1528as

003/august 1924/grammophon acoustic sessions in berlin

staatskapelle berlin/hans pfitzner

beethoven symphony no 4 in b flat op 60
377 ½ az   66245/69663
378az
379az   66246/69664
380az
381az   66247/69665
382az
385az   66248/69666
386az
383az   66249/69667
384az

004/october 1925/grammophon acoustic sessions in berlin

staatskapelle berlin/hans pfitzner

schumann symphony no 1 in b flat op 38 "spring"
2013as	66347/69795
2014 ½ as	
2015as	66348/69796
2016as	
2038as	66349/69797
2039as	
2040as	66350/69798
2041as	

005/february-march 1926/grammophon sessions in berlin using the pallophotophone (light-ray) system

staatskapelle berlin/hans pfitzner

schumann symphony no 2 in c op 61
2200as   66366/69828
2201as
2202as   66367/69829
2203as
2204as   66368/69830
2205as
2206as   66369/69831
2207as
2208as   66370/69832
2209as

pfitzner palestrina prelude
2212as   66121

pfitzner palestrina: act two prelude
2010as   66122
2011as

pfitzner palestrina: act three prelude
2042as   66132
2043as

006/1926/grammophon sessions in berlin

philharmonisches orchester berlin/hans pfitzner
orchestra described for these sessions as neues sinfonieorchester berlin

schumann symphony no 4 in d minor op 120

80 ½ bm	66410
81bm	
82bm	66411
83bm	
84bm	66412
85bm	
86bm	66413

007/1927/grammophon sessions in berlin

staatskapelle berlin/hans pfitzner

pfitzner palestrina prelude
203bi   66546

pfitzner palestrina: act two prelude
204 ½ bi   66547
205bi

pfitzner palestrina: act three prelude
206bi   66548
207bi

weber der freischütz overture
320bi   66545
321bi
322bi   66546

weber preciosa overture
323bi   66544/decca CA 8160
324bi

pfitzner die rose vom liebesgarten: trauermarsch
325bi   66557
326bi

pfitzner das christelflein overture
327bi   66606
328bi
329bi   66607

45: deutsche grammophon EPL 30 537
lp: heliodor 88 014
cd: emi 555 2252

45 and lp reissues incorrectly dated 1939

008/1928/grammophon sessions in berlin
hochschule für musik

philharmonisches orchester berlin/hans pfitzner

weber oberon overture
917bm   95091/brunswick 90042/decca CA 8015
918bm

mendelssohn hebrides overture
919bm   27292/decca CA 6093
929 bi I
lp: deutsche grammophon 2740 259

weber jubel overture
921 ½ bm   19858
922bm

009/1928/grammophon sessions in berlin

orchester der städtischen oper/hans pfitzner

beethoven symphony no 4 in b flat op 60

469be	95096/brunswick 90771
470be	
471 ½ be	95097/brunswick 90772
485be	
486be	95098/brunswick 90773
487be	
475be	95099/brunswick 90774
476be	
477be	95100/brunswick 90275
478be	

cd: naxos 8.110919

naxos incorrectly describes orchestra as staatskapelle berlin

beethoven symphony no 1 in c op 21

479be	95093
480 ½ be	
481be	95094
482be	
483be	95095
484be	

cd: naxos 8.110927

010/1928-1929/grammophon sessions in berlin

staatskapelle berlin/hans pfitzner

schumann symphony no 2 in c op 61

1464 ½ bm I	66873/95412/brunswick 90092
1465 ½ bm I	
1466bm I	66874/95413/brunswick 90093
1467 ½ bm I	
1468bm I	66875/95414/brunswick 90094
827 bi I	
1470 bm m	66876/95415/brunswick 90095
1471 bm m	
1472 bm I	66877/95416/brunswick 90096
1626 bm I	

lp: deutsche grammophon 2721 070 (second movement only)
cd: zyx music PD 50222 (second movement only)

pfitzner

011/1929/grammophon sessions in berlin
hochschule für musik

philharmonisches orchester berlin/hans pfitzner

beethoven symphony no 3 in e flat op 55 "eroica"

917 bi I	66939/brunswick 90060/decca CA 8047
918 bi I	
919 ½ bi I	66940/brunswick 90061/decca CA 8048
920 bi I	
921 bi I	66941/brunswick 90062/decca CA 8049
922 bi I	
923 bi I	66942/brunswick 90063/decca CA 8050
924 bi I	
925 ½ bi I	66943/brunswick 90064/decca CA 8051
926 bi I	
208 ½ bi I	66944/brunswick 90065/decca CA 8052
928 bi I	

cd: preiser 90201/naxos 8.110910

012/1929/grammophon sessions in berlin

staatskapelle berlin/hans pfitzner

mozart cosi fan tutte overture; le nozze di figaro overture
255 bs II   27066
256 bs II
cd: pristine PASC 305

lortzing zar und zimmermann overture
1627 bm I   27069
1628 bm I
cd: pristine PASC 305

013/1930/grammophon sessions in berlin

staatskapelle berlin/hans pfitzner

beethoven symphony no 6 in f op 68 "pastoral"
977 bi l   66467/95378/brunswick 90189/decca CA 8110
978 bi l
979 bi l   66468/95379/brunswick 90190/decca CA 8111
980 bi l
982 bi l   66469/95380/brunswick 90191/decca CA 8112
981 bi l
983 bi l   66470/95381/brunswick 90192/decca CA 8113
985 ½ bi l
986 bi l   66471/95382/brunswick 90193/decca CA 8114
987 bi l
988 bi l   66472/95383/Brunswick 90194/decca CA 8115
cd: naxos 8.110927

014/1931/grammophon sessions in berlin

staatskapelle berlin/hans pfitzner

pfitzner palestrina prelude
1148 ½ bi I   95459
1149 bi I
lp: heliodor 88 014
cd: emi 555 2252

pfitzner palestrina: act two prelude
1152 bi I   95460
1153 bi I
lp: heliodor 88 014
cd: emi 555 2252

pfitzner palestrina: act three prelude
1150 ½ bi I   95461
1151 bi I
lp: heliodor 88 014
cd: emi 555 2252

015/1932/grammophon sessions in berlin lützowstrasse studios

philharmonisches orchester berlin/hans pfitzner

pfitzner das herz: liebesmelodie
5292 ½ bd VIII   25273
5293 ½ bd VIII
lp: heliodor 88 014
cd: deutsche grammophon 459 0652
matrix numbers 5292 ½ bd VIII and 5293 ½ bd VII were replaced in 1939 by 3678 gn VIII and 3679 gn VIII

lanner pestherwalzer
5294 ½ bd VIII   25274/10133
5295 ½ bd VIII
cd: pristine PASC 305

016/1932/german radio recording

hans pfitzner, piano/heinrich rehkemper, baritone

schubert lieder: der doppelgänger; der jüngling an der quelle; die taubenpost
unpublished
german radio tape number 2988

pfitzner

017/9 november 1932/german radio recordings in breslau

schlesische philharmonie/hans pfitzner
*gisela derpsch, soprano

pfitzner das christelflein overture
474   unpublished
475
476
german radio tape numbers 2613/6200

*pfitzner orchesterlieder: sonst op 15 no 4;   verrat op 2 no 7
477   unpublished
478
german radio tape number 2975

pfitzner das käthchen von heilbronn: epilogue
479   unpublished
german radio tape number 3464

018/25 november 1932/german radio recordings in berlin

berliner funkorchester/hans pfitzner
*maria koerfer, piano

haydn symphony no 28 in a   hob I/28
2501   unpublished
2502
2503
2504
german radio tape numbers 2469/5986

*pfitzner piano concerto in e flat   op 31
2505   unpublished
2506
2507
2508
2509
2510
2511
2512
2513
2514
german radio tape numbers 2579/6105

019/1 april 1933/german radio recording of rehearsal in berlin

berliner funkorchester/hans pfitzner

beethoven symphony no 6 in f op 68 "pastoral"
304.0118   unpublished
304.0119
304.0120
304.0121
304.0122
304.0123
german radio tape number 4461

020/july 1933/grammophon sessions in berlin lützowstrasse studios

philharmonisches orchester berlin/hans pfitzner

beethoven symphony no 8 in f op 93
704 ½ be VIII   15020/67276
705 ½ be VIII
706 ½ be VIII   15021/67277
707 be VIII
708 be VIII   15022/67278
709 ½ be VIII
lp: past masters PM 31/deutsche grammophon 2740 259
cd: preiser 90221/naxos 8.110910

021/21 january 1934/reichsrundfunk recording in munich

orchester des reichsenders münchen/hans pfitzner

beethoven symphony no 6 in f op 68 "pastoral"
18121   unpublished
18122
18123
18124
18125
18126
18127
18128
18129
18130
18131
18132
reichsrundfunk tape numbers 2431/5950

022/7 may 1934/reichsrundfunk rehearsal recording in berlin

orchester des reichsenders berlin/hans pfitzner
else knepel, soprano/gerhard hüsch, baritone

pfitzner der arme heinrich: du bist wie eben kinder sind
19808   unpublished
19809
reichsrundfunk tape number 4462

023/1935/reichsrundfunk recording in berlin

orchester des reichsenders berlin/hans pfitzner

schumann symphony no 4 in d minor op 120

51461 unpublished
51462
51463
51464
51465
51466
51467

reichsrundfunk tape number 6029

024/29 june 1936/reichsrundfunk recording in munich

orchester des reichsenders münchen/hans pfitzner

bruch die loreley, arranged by pfitzner

31053 unpublished
31054
31055
31056
31057
31058
31059
31060
31061
31062
31063
31064

reichsrundfunk tape number 7183

025/19 march 1937/reichsrundfunk recording in munich

orchester des reichsenders münchen/hans pfitzner
julius patzak, tenor

pfitzner die rose vom liebesgarten: erzählung vom liebesgarten
35671			unpublished
35672
reichsrundfunk tape number 7191

026/february 1938/electrola sessions in berlin

staatskapelle berlin/hans pfitzner
max strub, violin/ludwig hoelscher, cello

pfitzner duo for violin, cello and orchestra op 43
2RA 2633		DB 4508
2RA 2634
2RA 2635		DB 4509
2RA 2636
lp: E 60802/WDLP 703
cd: preiser 90029/emi 555 2252

027/february 1938/electrola sessions in berlin

hans pfitzner, piano/gerhard hüsch, baritone

pfitzner lied: hast du von den fischerkindern
ORA 2639 DA 4439/DA 4475
lp: E 60051/WDLP 566/preiser LV 208
cd: emi 555 2252/preiser 89519/90029

pfitzner lieder: herbstgefühl; leuchtende tage
ORA 2640 DA 4439
lp: preiser LV 208
cd: emi 555 2252/preiser 89519/90029

pfitzner lieder: hussens kerker; säerspruch
ORA 2637 unpublished
ORA 2638
lp: preiser LV 208
cd: emi 555 2252/preiser 89519/90029

pfitzner lied: michaelskirchplatz
ORA 2638 unpublished
lp: preiser LV 208
cd: preiser 89519

028/16 february 1939/reichsrundfunk recording in berlin

orchester des reichsenders berlin/hans pfitzner
*ludwig hoelscher, cello

pfitzner das käthchen von heilbronn overture
51448   unpublished
51449
51450
reichsrundfunk tape number 6201

***pfitzner cello concerto no 2 in g op 42**
51451   unpublished
51452
51453
51454
51455
51456
reichsrundfunk tape number 6107

pfitzner die rose vom liebesgarten: blütenwunder und trauermarsch
51457   unpublished
51458
reichsrundfunk tape number 7292

029/december 1939/electrola sessions in berlin

hans pfitzner, piano/gerhard hüsch, baritone

pfitzner lieder: in danzig; abbitte
ORA 4373   DA 4477
ORA 4370
lp: E 60051/WDLP 566/preiser LV 208
cd: emi 555 2252/preiser 89519/90029

pfitzner lieder: der einsame; der gärtner
ORA 4371   DA 4476
ORA 4377
lp: E 60051/WDLP 566/preiser LV 208
cd: emi 555 2252/preiser 89519/90029

pfitzner lieder: nachts
ORA 4376   DA 4478
lp: E 60051/WDLP 566/preiser LV 208
cd: emi 555 2252/preiser 89519/90029

pfitzner lied: zum abschied meiner tochter
ORA 4375   DA 4439/DA 4475
lp: E 60051/WDLP 566/preiser LV 208
cd: emi 555 2252/preiser 89519/90029

030/21 september 1940/grammophon sessions in berlin alte jakobstrasse studios

philharmonisches orchester berlin/hans pfitzner

pfitzner symphony no 2 in c op 46

1519 gs IX	67604
1520 ½ gs IX	
1521 ½ gs IX	67605
1522 ½ gs IX	
1523 gs IX	67606

lp: heliodor 88 014
cd: preiser 90029

031/20-22 april 1942/kristall sessions in vienna

wiener philharmoniker/hans pfitzner

weber der freischütz: overture and entr'acte

032/11-13 december 1944/reichsrundfunk recording in vienna musikvereinssaal

wiener philharmoniker/hans pfitzner

pfitzner das käthchen von heilbronn overture
lp: urania URLP 7050/varese sarabande VC 81094

HANS PFITZNER: COMPOSER DISCOGRAPHY
session numbers enable cross-reference to the main chronological discography

LUDWIG VAN BEETHOVEN (1770-1827)
symphony no 1 in c op 21
009/berlin 1928

symphony no 3 in e flat op 55 "eroica"
011/berlin 1929

symphony no 4 in b flat op 60
003/berlin 1924   009/berlin 1928

symphony no 6 in f op 68 "pastoral"
001/berlin 1923   013/berlin 1930
019/berlin 1933   021/berlin 1934

symphony no 7: abridged versions of second and fourth movements
001/berlin 1923

symphony no 8 in f op 93
020/berlin 1933

symphony no 8: second movement
001/berlin 1923

composer discography/continued

MAX BRUCH (1838-1920)
die loreley, arranged by pfitzner
024/munich 1936

FRANZ JOSEF HAYDN (1732-1809)
symphony no 28 in a hob I/28
018/berlin 1932

JOSEF LANNER (1801-1843)
pestherwalzer
015/berlin 1932

ALBERT LORTZING (1801-1851)
zar und zimmermann overture
012/berlin 1929

composer discography/continued

FELIX MENDELSSOHN-BARTHOLDY (1809-1847)
hebrides overture
008/berlin 1928

WOLFGANG AMADEUS MOZART (1756-1791)
cosi fan tutte overture
012/berlin 1929

le nozze di figaro overture
012/berlin 1929

HANS PFITZNER (1869-1949)
symphony no 2 in c op 46
030/berlin 1940

cello concerto no 2 in g op 42
028.berlin 1939

duo for violin, cello and orchestra op 43
026/berlin 1938

piano concerto in e flat op 31
018/berlin 1932

composer discography/continued

pfitzner der arme heinrich: du bist wie eben kinder sind
022/berlin 1934

das christelflein overture
001/berlin 1923   007/berlin 1927
017/breslau 1932

das fest auf solhaug: overture and act two finale
001/berlin 1923

das herz: liebesmelodie
015/berlin 1932

das käthchen von heilbronn overture
028/berlin 1939   032/vienna 1944

composer discography/continued

pfitzner das käthchen von heilbronn: epilogue
001/berlin 1923   017/breslau 1932

das käthchen von heilbronn: march
001/berlin 1923

lieder
027/berlin 1938   029/berlin 1939

orchesterlieder
017/breslau 1932

palestrina: the three preludes
005/berlin 1926   007/berlin 1927
014/berlin 1931

die rose vom liebesgarten: trauermarsch
001/berlin 1923   007/berlin 1927
028/berlin 1939

composer discography/continued

pfitzner die rose vom liebesgarten: erzählung vom liebesgarten
025/munich 1937

pfitzner die rose vom liebesgarten: blütenwunder
028/berlin 1939

FRANZ SCHUBERT (1797-1928)
lieder
016/1932

ROBERT SCHUMANN (1810-1856)
symphony no 1 in b flat op 38 "spring"
004/berlin 1925

symphony no 2 in c op 61
005/berlin 1926   010/berlin 1928-1929

symphony no 4 in d minor op 120
001/berlin 1923   006/berlin 1926
023/berlin 1935

composer discography/concluded
CARL MARIA VON WEBER (1778-1826)
der freischütz overture
001/berlin 1923   007/berlin 1927
031/vienna 1942

der freischütz: entr'acte
031/vienna 1942

jubel overture
008/berlin 1928

oberon overture
008/berlin 1928

preciosa overture
002/berlin 1924   007/berlin 1927

OSKAR FRIED: CHRONOLOGICAL DISCOGRAPHY

001/1923/grammophon acoustic sessions in berlin

staatskapelle berlin/oskar fried
*berliner domchor/gertrud bindernagel, soprano/
emmi leisner, contralto

*mahler symphony no 2 in c minor "resurrection"

371az	66290/69681
370az	
1552as	66291/69682
372az	
1554as	66292/69683
1555as	
1556as	66293/69684
1557as	
1558as	66294/69685
1559as	
1560as	66295/69686
1567 ½ as	
373az	66296/69687
1553as	
1561as	66297/69688
1562as	
1564as	66298/69689
1563 ½ as	

001/1923/mahler symphony no 2/concluded
322 ½ az   66299/69690
374 az
375 az   66300/69691
376 az
lp: discocorp BWS 719/pearl OPAL 821-822
cd: pearl GEMMCDS 9929/membran 222145.444/
naxos 8.110152-110153/symposium 1337
(fourth movement only)

brahms symphony no 1 in c minor op 68
507az   66304/69701
508az
509az   66305/69702
512az
511az   66306/69703
513az
515az   66307/69704
516az
517az   66308/69705
lp: past masters PM 32

fried

002/1923-1924/vox acoustic sessions in berlin

vox-sinfonieorchester/oskar fried

bizet carmen: acts three and four preludes
1355A   01471
1356 ½ A

bizet l'arlesienne: suite no 1
1357A   01472
1358A
1366A   01475
1367A

liszt hungarian rhapsody no 2 in c sharp minor
1368A   01478
1369A

jaap kool adagio aus der arbeitersinfonie
1392A   01480
1393 ½ A

002/1923-1924/vox sessions in berlin/concluded

liszt hungarian rhapsody no 1 in f minor

       01473

       01474

strauss der rosenkavalier waltz, arranged by otto singer

       01479

weber aufforderung zum tanz

       01481

fried fantasy on humperdinck's hänsel und gretel

       01519

       01520

003/1924/grammophon acoustic sessions in berlin

staatskapelle berlin/oskar fried

fried fantasy on verdi's aida

493az	65940
494az	
495az	65941
496az	
497az	65942
498az	

weber oberon overture

501az	65938
502az	

003/1924/grammophon sessions in berlin/continued

beethoven symphony no 3 in e flat op 55 "eroica"

1600as	66239/69706
1601as	
1602as	66240/69707
1603as	
1604as	66241/69708
1605as	
1606as	66242/69709
1607 ½ as	
1608 ½ as	66243/69710
1609as	
1610as	66244/69711
1611as	

lp: rarissima 43
cd: music and arts CD 1185/arbiter 140

leoncavallo i pagliacci: potpourri

1617as II	65939
1618as II	

gounod faust: ballet music

1619as	65971
1620as	
1621as	65972
1622as	

004/november 1925/grammophon acoustic sessions in berlin

staatskapelle berlin/oskar fried

bruckner symphony no 7 in e

1716as	66318/69753
1717as	
1718as	66319/69754
1727as	
565 ½ as	66320/69755
566as	
570 ½ as	66321/69756
571as	
572as	66322/69757
1703as	
1704as	66323/69758
1728as	
1735as	66324/69759
1736as	

lp: discocorp BWS 719
cd: music and arts CD 1231/wing WCD 61

005/1925/grammophon acoustic sessions in berlin

staatskapelle berlin/oskar fried

stravinsky firebird suite
1917 ½ as   66337/69776
1930 ½ as
1931 ½ as   66338/69777
1932 ½ as
cd: music and arts CD 1198

beethoven könig stephan overture
1979 ½ as   66119
1980as
cd: arbiter 140

boieldieu le caliphe de bagdad overture
1981as   66211
1982as

liszt mazeppa
2000as   66117
2001as
2002as   66118
2003as
cd: music and arts CD 1185

fried

**006/october-november 1925/grammophon
acoustic sessions in berlin**

staatskapelle berlin/oskar fried

berlioz symphonie fantastique
2030 ½ as	69808
2031 ½ as	
2033as	69809
838 ½ az	
2009as	69810
836az	
2032as	69811

this recording omitted the fourth movement

beethoven symphony no 2 in d op 36
2048 ½ as	66235
2049 ½ as	
2050as	66236
2051as	
2052as	66237
884 ½ az	
885az	66238
886az	

lp: past masters PM 17
cd: music and arts CD 1198

007/1925-1926/grammophon sessions in berlin

staatskapelle berlin/oskar fried

strauss eine alpensinfonie op 64

2138 ½ as	66351/69803
2139as	
2140as	66352/69804
2141as	
2142as	66353/69805
2143as	
2145 ½ as	66354/69806
2163as	
2164as	66355/69807

lp: rarissima 19
cd: music and arts CD 1167

fried

007/1925-26/grammophon sessions in berlin/concluded

berlioz symphonie fantastique

2030 ½ as	66356
2031 ½ as	
2033as	66367
838 ½ az	
2222as	66358
2224as	
2223as	66359
2009 ½ as	
836az	66360
2032as	

this was a re-recording of the work, but now with all five movements and using the same matrix numbers as the earlier recording (session number 006)

mozart serenade no 13 in g K525 "eine kleine nachtmusik"

222 ½ bg	66364/69826
223 ½ bg	
229bg	66365/69827
230bg	

008/1927/grammophon sessions in berlin

staatskapelle/*staatsopernchor/oskar fried

***mascagni cavalleria rusticana: regina coeli**
157bi   66517
cd: music and arts CD 1231

***wagner tannhäuser: pilgerchor**
169bi   66516
cd: music and arts CD 1231

***weber der freischütz: jägerchor**
170bi   66518
cd: music and arts CD 1231/arbiter 153

***wagner lohengrin: brautchor**
171bi   66517
cd: music and arts CD 1231

fried

008/1927/grammophon sessions in berlin/concluded
*wagner tannhäuser: einzug der gäste
172bi   66516
cd: music and arts CD 1231/arbiter 153

*wagner der fliegende holländer: spinnchor
173bi   66518
cd: music and arts CD 1231

tchaikovsky casse noisette: suite from the ballet
326be   95030/90416/516656/decca CA 8132
327be
329be   95031/90417/516657/decca CA 8133
330be
331be   95032/90418/516658/decca CA 8134
332be
cd: dante LYS 200

009/1927/grammophon sessions in berlin

philharmonisches orchester berlin/oskar fried

stravinsky firebird suite
853 ½ bm   95052/90419/516650/decca CA 8235
854bm
855bm   95053/90420/516651/decca CA 8236
856 ½ bm
lp: deutsche grammophon 2721 070/2740 259/
discocorp BWS 719
cd: dante LYS 386/koch 3-7146-2/arbiter 153/
zyx music PD 50252

010/1927-1928/grammophon sessions in berlin

staatskapelle berlin/oskar fried

gounod faust: valse
142be   19804/516249/decca LY 6038

thomas mignon overture
241be   19744
242be

adam si j'etais roi overture
243be   19743
248be

suppe dichter und bauer overture
249be   19739
250be

011/1928/grammophon sessions in berlin

orchester der städtischen oper/oskar fried

offenbach les contes d'hoffmann: barcarolle
443be   19804/566249/decca LY 6038

rossini la gazza ladra overture
452be   19805
453 ½ be
cd: arbiter 153

012/1928/grammophon sessions in berlin

staatskapelle berlin/oskar fried

mozart serenade no 13 in g K525 "eine kleine nachtmusik"
922be				66669/90144
923be
924be				66670/90145
925be
cd: arbiter 153 (925be only)

wagner faust overture
1390bm I			95318/90077
1391bm I
681bi I			95319/90078
cd: music and arts CD 1167

donizetti don pasquale overture
1400bm I			27003
1401bm I

013/1928/grammophon sessions in berlin hochschule für musik

philharmonisches orchester berlin/oskar fried

liszt mazeppa

1267bm	66787/90165/decca CA 8177
1268 ½ bm	
1269bm I	66788/90166/decca CA 8178
1340bm I	

lp: discocorp BWS 734
cd: koch 3-7146-2/music and arts CD 1185

liszt les preludes

1341bm I	66812/90163/decca CA 8166
1342bm I	
1343bm I	66813/90164/decca CA 8167
1344bm I	

cd: koch 3-7146-2/music and arts CD 1185

fried

013/1928/grammophon sessions in berlin/concluded
grieg peer gynt: suites one and two
                95033/516608

                95034/516609

                95035/516610

                95036/516611

rimsky-korsakov scheherazade
1359bm I	95187/90361
1360 ½ bm I	
1361bm I	95188/90362
1362bm I	
1363 ½ bm I	95189/90363
1364 ½ bm I	
1365bm I	95190/90364
1366bm I	
1387 ½ bm I	95191/90365
1388 ½ bm I	
1389bm I	95192/90366

cd: koch 3-7146-2/dante LYS 386

014/6-11 october 1928/grammophon sessions in berlin hochschule für musik

philharmonisches orchester berlin/oskar fried

weber euryanthe overture
205bs I   19988
206bs I
lp: deutsche grammophon 2740 259
cd: music and arts CD 1198

fried fantasy on humperdinck's hänsel und gretel
1416bm I   19984
1417bm I
1418bm I   19985
1419bm I
cd: music and arts CD 1167

saint-saens danse macabre
1420 ½ bm   95204/92094
1421 ½ bm
lp: deutsche grammophon 2740 259
cd: dante LYS 280/arbiter 153

015/1-6 february 1929/columbia sessions in london westminster central hall

orchestra of the royal philharmonic society/oskar fried

tchaikovsky symphony no 6 in b minor op 64 "pathetique"
WAX 4620   9867/columbia (usa) M 119
WAX 4621
WAX 4622   9868/columbia (usa) M 119
WAX 4623
WAX 4624   9869/columbia (usa) M 119
WAX 4629
WAX 4630   9870/columbia (usa) M 119
WAX 4631
WAX 4632   9871/columbia (usa) M 119
WAX 4633
cd: dante LYS 200/preiser 90326

tchaikovsky casse noisette: suite from the ballet
WAX 4634   L 2318
WAX 4635
WAX 4636   L 2319
WAX 4637
WAX 4638   L 2320
WAX 4639
cd: preiser 90326

016/1929/grammophon sessions in berlin

staatskapelle berlin/bruno-kittel-chor/oskar fried lotte leonard, soprano/jenny sonnenberg, contralto/eugene transky, tenor/wilhelm guttmann, bass-baritone

beethoven symphony no 9 in d minor op 125 "choral"

633bm	66657/brunswick 90179
634bm	
635bm	66658/brunswick 90180
585 ¾ bm	
636bm	66659/brunswick 90181
637bm	
638bm	66660/brunswick 90182
639 ½ bm	
586 ½ bm	66661/brunswick 90183
587bm	
566 ½ bm	66662/brunswick 90184
564 ½ bm	
565 ½ bm	66663/brunswick 90185
567 ½ bm	

lp: melodiya 031237-031238
cd: pearl GEMMCD 9372/iron needle IN 1395/ dante LYS 279/naxos 8.110929

017/1930/columbia session in london westminster central hall

british symphony orchestra/oskar fried

delibes coppelia: suite from the ballet
AX 5836   LX 114/LFX 171
AX 5837
AX 5838   LX 115/LFX 172
AX 5839
cd: preiser 90326

018/1 february 1936/acetate from a bbc broadcast in london queen's hall

bbc symphony orchestra/oskar fried
astra desmond, contralto

mahler das lied von der erde: von der schönheit
cd: arbiter 153
sung in english; last eight bars missing

019/1937/radio broadcast in moscow

all-union radio orchestra/oskar fried

mozart symphony no 40 in g minor K550
cd: arbiter 153

020/1937/radio broadcast in moscow

ussr state symphony orchestra/oskar fried

berlioz symphonie fantastique
lp: melodiya 031239-031240/ariola 88329XAK
cd: dante LYS 280

OSKAR FRIED: COMPOSER DISCOGRAPHY

session numbers enable cross-reference to the main chronological discography

ADOLPHE ADAM (1803-1856)
si j'etais roi overture
010/berlin 1927-1928

LUDWIG VAN BEETHOVEN (1770-1827)
symphony no 2 in d op 36
006/berlin 1925

symphony no 3 in e flat op 55 "eroica"
003/berlin 1924

symphony no 9 in d minor op 125 "choral"
016/berlin 1929

könig stephan overture
005/berlin 1925

HECTOR BERLIOZ (1803-1869)
symphonie fantastique
006/berlin 1925   007/berlin 1925-1926
020/moscow 1937

composer discography/continued

GEORGES BIZET (1838-1875)
l'arlesienne: suite no 1
002/berlin 1923-1924

carmen: preludes to acts three and four
002/berlin 1923-1924

FRANCOIS BOIELDIEU (1775-1834)
le caliphe de bagdad overture
005/berlin 1925

JOHANNES BRAHMS (1833-1897)
symphony no 1 in c minor op 68
001/berlin 1923

ANTON BRUCKNER (1824-1896)
symphony no 7 in e
004/berlin 1924

composer discography/continued

LEO DELIBES (1836-1891)
sylvia: ballet suite
017/london 1930

GAETONO DONIZETTI (1797-1848)
don pasquale overture
012/berlin 1928

OSKAR FRIED (1874-1941)
fantasy on humperdinck's hänsel und gretel
002/berlin 1923-1924   014/berlin 1928

fantasy on verdi's aida
003/berlin 1924

CHARLES GOUNOD (1818-1893)
faust: ballet music
003/berlin 1924

faust: valse
010/berlin 1927-1928

composer discography/continued

EDVARD GRIEG (1843-1907)
peer gynt: orchestral suites 1 and 2
013/berlin 1928

JAAP KOOL (1891-1950)
adagio aus der arbeitersinfonie
002/berlin 1923-1924

RUGGIERO LEONCAVALLO (1858-1918)
i pagliacci: potpourri
003/berlin 1924

composer discography/continued

FRANZ LISZT (1811-1886)
hungarian rhapsody no 1
002/berlin 1923-1924

hungarian rhapsody no 2
002/berlin 1923-1924

mazeppa
005/berlin 1925   013/berlin 1928

les preludes
013/berlin 1928

GUSTAV MAHLER (1860-1911)
symphony no 2 "resurrection"
001/berlin 1923

das lied von der erde: von der schönheit
018/london 1936

PIETRO MASCAGNI (1863-1945)
cavalleria rusticana: regina coeli
008/berlin 1927

composer discography/continued

WOLFGANG AMADEUS MOZART (1756-1791)
symphony no 40 in g minor K550
019/moscow 1937

eine kleine nachtmusik K525
007/berlin 1925-1926   012/berlin 1928

JACQUES OFFENBACH (1819-1880)
les contes d'hoffmann: barcarolle
011/berlin 1928

NIKOLAI RIMSKY-KORSAKOV (1844-1908)
scheherazade
013/berlin 1928

composer discography/continued

GIOACCHINO ROSSINI (1792-1868)
la gazza ladra overture
011/berlin 1928

CAMILLE SAINT-SAENS (1835-1921)
danse macabre
014/berlin 1928

RICHARD STRAUSS (1864-1949)
eine alpensinfonie op 64
007/berlin 1925-1926

der rosenkavalier: waltz arranged by singer
002/berlin 1923-1924

IGOR STRAVINSKY (1882-1962)
firebird suite
005/berlin 1925   009/berlin 1927

composer discography/continued

FRANZ VON SUPPE (1819-1895)
dichter und bauer overture
010/berlin 1927-1928

PIOTR TCHAIKOVSKY (1840-1893)
symphony no 6 in b minor op 64 "pathetique"
015/london 1929

casse noisette: ballet suite
008/berlin 1927   015/london 1929

AMBROISE THOMAS (1811-1896)
mignon overture
010/berlin 1927-1928

composer discography/concluded
RICHARD WAGNER (1813-1883)
a faust overture
012/berlin 1928

der fliegende holländer: spinnchor
008/berlin 1927

lohengrin: brautchor
008/berlin 1927

tannhäuser: einzug der gäste
008/berlin 1927

tannhäuser: pilgerchor
008/berlin 1927

CARL MARIA VON WEBER (1786-1826)
aufforderung zum tanz
002/berlin 1923-1924

euryanthe overture
014/berlin 1928

der freischütz: jägerchor
008/berlin 1927

oberon overture
003/berlin 1924

OSWALD KABASTA: CHRONOLOGICAL DISCOGRAPHY

001/19 february 1936/ravag radio recording in vienna rosenhügel studio

wiener symphoniker/oswald kabasta
franz schmidt, piano

mozart concert rondo in a K386
this recording remains unpublished

002/19 may 1938/reichsrundfunk recording in munich

orchester des reichsenders münchen/
oswald kabasta

falla el sombrero de 3 picos: danza espanol
this recording remains unpublished

003/18 january 1939/electrola sessions in berlin philharmonie

münchner philharmoniker/oswald kabasta

respighi impressioni brasiliane
2RA 3559   DB 4643
2RA 3560
2RA 3561   DB 4644
2RA 3562
cd: musica classica 2009-2010/dante LYS 419-424

verdi la forza del destino overture
2RA 3563   DB 4642
2RA 3564
lp: past masters PM 25
cd: musica classica 2009-2010/dante LYS 419-424

falla el sombrero de 3 picos: danza espanol
matrix and catalogue numbers could not be traced

004/25 january 1939/reichsrundfunk recordings in vienna musikvereinssaal

wiener philharmoniker/oswald kabasta

weber oberon overture; johann strauss kaiserwalzer; schubert 5 deutsche tänze
these recordings remain unpublished

005/3 march 1939/reichsrundfunk recording in munich

orchester des reichsenders münchen/oswald kabasta

mozart symphony no 35 in d K385 "haffner"
this recording, of which only the second and third movements survive, remains unpublished

006/probably 1940/columbia session in vienna konzerthaus

wiener symphoniker/oswald kabasta

haydn arranged by komzak deutschlandlied
based on second movement of string quartet op 76 no 3
WHA 550   DV 1061
cd: musica classica 2009-2010/dante LYS 419-424

**007/2 march 1940/electrola sessions in berlin
beethovensaal der philharmonie**

münchner philharmoniker/oswald kabasta
*rudolf schöne, violin

***wagner träume from wesendonk-lieder
arranged for violin and orchestra; albumblatt
arranged for violin and orchestra**
2RA 4500   DB 5573
2RA 4501
lp: past masters PM 25
cd: musica classica 2009-2010/dante LYS 419-424

schubert symphony no 3 in d D200
2RA 4506   DB 5575
2RA 4507
2RA 4503   DB 5576
2RA 4502
2RA 4504   DB 5577
2RA 4505
lp: emi 1C137 53032-53036
cd: musica classica 2009-2010/preiser 90303/
dante LYS 419-424

007/2 march 1940/electrola sessions in berlin/
concluded

ernst von dohnanyi sinfonische minuten op 36

2RA 4508   DB 5591
2RA 4509
2RA 4510   DB 5592
2RA 4511

lp: past masters PM 25
cd: musica classica 2009-2010/dante LYS 419-424

dvorak waldesruhe for cello and orchestra
matrix and catalogue numbers could not be traced

008/30 september 1940/reichsrundfunk recording in stuttgart

orchester des reichsenders stuttgart/
oswald kabasta

mozart symphony no 41 in c K551 "jupiter"
this recording, of which only the first and second movements survive, remains unpublished

**009/may 1941/electrola sessions in munich
deutsches museum**

münchner philharmoniker/oswald kabasta
*rudolf schöne, violin

beethoven symphony no 8 in f op 93
2RA 5000   DB 5639
2RA 5001
2RA 5002   DB 5640
2RA 5003
2RA 5004   DB 5641
2RA 5005
cd: musica classica 2009-2010/dante LYS 419-424

beethoven coriolan overture op 62
2RA 5006   DB 5636
2RA 5007
lp: past masters PM 25
cd: musica classica 2009-2010/dante LYS 419-424

009/may 1941/electrola sessions in munich/concluded
*mozart serenata notturna K239: rondo
2RA 5010   DB 5651
cd: dante LYS 419-424

mozart symphony no 41 in c K551 "jupiter"
2RA 5013   DB 5648
2RA 5014
2RA 5022   DB 5649
2RA 5023
2RA 5015   DB 5650
2RA 5011
2RA 5012   DB 5651
cd: musica classica 2009-2010/preiser 90303/
dante LYS 419-424

010/21 september 1941/reichsrundfunk recordings in vienna musikvereinssaal

wiener philharmoniker/oswald kabasta
*willi boskovsky, violin/*walter barylli, violin

mozart symphony no 25 in g minor K183;
*mozart concertone in c for 2 violins K190
these recordings remain unpublished

011/24-25 september 1942/electrola sessions in vienna konzerthaus

münchner philharmoniker/oswald kabasta

bruckner symphony no 7 in e

2RA 5638	DB 7684
2RA 5639	
2RA 5640	DB 7685
2RA 5641	
2RA 5642	DB 7686
2RA 5643	
2RA 5644	DB 7687
2RA 5645	
2RA 5646	DB 7688
2RA 5647	
2RA 5648	DB 7689
2RA 5649	
2RA 5650	DB 7690
2RA 5651	
2RA 5652	DB 7691
2RA 5653	

lp: emi 1C053 28981
cd: musica classica 2007-2008/preiser 90308/ dante LYS 419-424/emi 566 2102

011/24-25 september 1942/electrola sessions in vienna/concluded

berger legende vom prinzen eugen

2RA 5666   DB 7652
2RA 5667
lp: past masters PM 25
cd: musica classica 2009-2010/dante LYS 419-424

012/1942-1943/reichsrundfunk recording in vienna konzerthaus

wiener symphoniker/oswald kabasta

schubert symphony no 5 in b flat D485
cd: preiser 90303/music and arts CD 969/
dante LYS 419-424

013/7 june 1943/reichsrundfunk recording in munich deutsches museum

münchner philharmoniker/oswald kabasta

bruckner symphony no 9 in d minor
cd: music and arts CD 969/dante LYS 419-424

014/19-20 june 1943/reichsrundfunk recording in munich deutsches museum

münchner philharmoniker/oswald kabasta

beethoven symphony no 3 in e flat op 55 "eroica"
cd: music and arts CD 969/CD 1072/
dante LYS 419-424

015/30 june 1943/reichsrundfunk recording in munich deutsches museum

münchner philharmoniker/oswald kabasta

bruckner symphony no 4 in e flat "romantic"
cd: arkadia 78527/pilz acanta 78005/musica classica 2007-2008/music and arts CD 1072/
dante LYS 419-424

016/14 july 1944/reichsrundfunk recording in munich deutsches museum

münchner philharmoniker/oswald kabasta

dvorak symphony no 9 in e minor op 95 "from the new world"
lp: relief REL 813
cd: relief CR 1813/as-disc AS 111/dante LYS 419-424/music and arts CD 1072
relief and as-disc editions were incorrectly attributed to wilhelm furtwängler

017/16 september 1944/reichsrundfunk recording in munich deutsches museum

münchner philharmoniker/oswald kabasta
arthur troester, cello

schumann cello concerto in a minor op 129
this recording remains unpublished

OSWALD KABASTA: COMPOSER DISCOGRAPHY
session numbers enable cross-reference to the main chronological discography

LUDWIG VAN BEETHOVEN (1770-1827)
symphony no 3 in e flat op 55 "eroica"
014/munich 1943

symphony no 8 in f op 93
009/munich 1941

coriolan overture op 62
009/munich 1941

THEODOR BERGER (1905-1992)
legende vom prinzen eugen
011/vienna 1942

composer discography/continued

ANTON BRUCKNER (1824-1896)
symphony no 4 in e flat "romantic"
015/munich 1943

symphony no 7 in e
011/vienna 1942

symphony no 9 in d minor
013/munich 1943

ERNST VON DOHNANYI (1877-1960)
sinfonische minuten
007/berlin 1940

ANTONIN DVORAK (1841-1904)
symphony no 9 in e minor op 95 "new world"
016/munich 1944

waldesruhe for cello and orchestra
007/berlin 1940

composer discography/continued

MANUEL DE FALLA (1876-1946)
el sombrero de 3 picos: danza espanol
002/munich 1938   003/berlin 1939

FRANZ JOSEF HAYDN (1732-1809)
deutschlandlied, arranged by komzak from string quartet op 76 no 3
006/vienna 1940

WOLFGANG AMADEUS MOZART (1756-1791)
symphony no 25 in g minor K183
010/vienna 1941

symphony no 35 in d K385 "haffner"
004/munich 1939

symphony no 41 in c K551 "jupiter"
008/stuttgart 1940   009/munich 1941

rondo in d for piano and orchestra K386
001/vienna 1936

concertone for 2 violins and orchestra K190
010/vienna 1941

serenata notturna K239: rondo
009/munich 1941

composer discography/continued

OTTORINO RESPIGHI (1879-1936)
impressioni brasiliane
003/berlin 1939

FRANZ SCHUBERT (1797-1828)
symphony no 3 in d D200
007/berlin 1940

symphony no 5 in b flat K485
012/vienna 1942-1943

5 deutsche tänze
004/vienna 1939

ROBERT SCHUMANN (1810-1856)
cello concerto in a minor op 129
017/munich 1944

composer discography/concluded

JOHANN STRAUSS II (1825-1899)
kaiserwalzer
004/vienna 1939

GIUSEPPE VERDI (1813-1901)
la forza del destino overture
003/berlin 1939

RICHARD WAGNER (1813-1883)
albumblatt, arranged for violin and orchestra
007/berlin 1940

wesendonk-lieder: träume, arranged for violin and orchestra
007/berlin 1940

CARL MARIA VON WEBER (1786-1826)
oberon overture
004/vienna 1939

KARL MUCK : CHRONOLOGICAL DISCOGRAPHY

001/2-5 october 1917/victor acoustic sessions in the executive office building of the victor talking machine company in camden new jersey

boston symphony orchestra/karl muck

tchaikovsky symphony no 4: fourth movement
C 20815   74553/6050
C 20816   74554/6050
lp: SRL 12-11
cd: bso classics 171002

wolf-ferrari il segreto di susanna overture
B 20817   unpublished
cd: bso classics 171002

wagner lohengrin: act three prelude
B 20818   64744/547
lp: LM 2651/boston symphony orchestra 0118.237
cd: bso classics 171002/naxos 8.110858

001/1917/victor acoustic sessions/concluded

berlioz la damnation de faust: marche hongroise
C 20819   unpublished
cd: bso classics 171002

beethoven symphony no 7: first part of fourth movement
B 20820   unpublished
B 20821
cd: bso classics 171002 (B 20820 only)

tchaikovsky casse noisette: valse des fleurs
C 20822   unpublished
cd: bso classics 171002

berlioz la damnation de faust: ballet des sylphes
B 20823   unpublished
cd: bso classics 171002

tckaikovsky orchestral suite no 1: marche miniature
B 20824   64766/547
cd: rca-bmg 09026 638612/bso classics 171002

002/august 1927/columbia sessions in bayreuth festspielhaus

orchester und chor der bayreuther festspiele/karl muck
*ingeborg holmgren/anny helm/minnie ruske-leopold/
hilde sinnek/maria nezadal/charlotte müller

wagner parsifal: verwandlungsmusik und gralsszene (geleiten wir den bergenden schrein.....zum letzten liebesmahle)

WAX 3010	L 2007/CLX 12515/M 337
WAX 3011	
WAX 3012	L 2008/CLX 12516/M 337
WAX 3013	
WAX 3014	L 2009/CLX 12517/M 337
WAX 3015	
WAX 3016	L 2010/CLX 12518/M 337
WAX 3017	

lp: QCX 10464/pearl OPAL 837-838/
melodiya M10 42887-42888/discocorp
IGI 379 (gralsszene only)/emi
1C137 71174-71175M (gralsszene only)/
1C049 30679M (gralsszene only)/
1C181 30669-30678M (gralsszene only)
cd: pearl GEMMCD 9843/gebhardt JGCD 0063
(gralsszene only)/malibran CDRG 134/preiser
90393/naxos 8.110049-110050

IGI 379 was incorrectly described as a live 1933 recording from bayreuth

002/august 1927/columbia sessions in bayreuth/ concluded

*wagner parsifal: blumenmädchenszene (komm holder knabe!)

WAX 3018   L 2011/CLX 12519/GQX 10477/M 337
WAX 3019
lp: QCX 10464/electrola E 83387/pearl OPAL 837-838/ melodiya M10 42887-42888/emi 1C137 78174-78175M/ 1C181 30669-30678M
cd: pearl GEMMCD 9843/malibran CDRG 134/ preiser 90393/naxos 8.110049-110050

the complete set of 1927 bayreuth recordings, also including items conducted by franz von hoesslin and siegfried wagner, was also published in the columbia international series

003/8-11 december 1927/electrola sessions in berlin singakademie

staatskapelle berlin/karl muck

wagner die meistersinger von nürnberg overture
CWR 1402   EJ 223/victor 6858
CWR 1403
CWR 1404   EJ 224/victor 6859
cd: preiser 90269/centaur CRC 2142/appian APR 5521/symposium 1345/naxos 8.110858

wagner götterdämmerung: siegfrieds rheinfahrt und trauermarsch
CWR 1418   EJ 224/D 1525/victor 6859
CWR 1419   EJ 225/D 1585/victor 6860
CWR 1420
lp: melodiya M10 42887-42888
cd: preiser 90269/centaur CRC 2142/appian APR 5521/naxos 8.110858 (rheinfahrt only)/symposium 1345

wagner parsifal prelude
CWR 1421   EJ 226/D 1400/victor 6861
CWR 1422
CWR 1423   EJ 227/D 1401/victor 6862
CWR 1424
cd: pearl GEMMCDS 9843/preiser 90269/centaur CRC 2142/naxos 8.110049-110050/appian APR 5521

004/15 may 1928/electrola sessions in berlin singakademie

staatskapelle berlin/karl muck

wagner tristan und isolde prelude
CLR 4129   EJ 366/D 2028
CLR 4130
CLR 4131   EJ 367/D 2029
cd: preiser 90269/centaur CRC 2142/appian APR 5521/symposium 1345/naxos 8.110858

wagner der fliegende holländer overture
CLR 4132   EJ 368/D 2027
CLR 4133
CLR 4134   EJ 367/D 2028
lp: melodiya M10 42887-42888
cd: preiser 90269/centaur CRC 2142/appian APR 5521/symposium 1345/naxos 8.110858

wagner tannhäuser overture
CLR 4135   EJ 335
CLR 4136
CLR 4137   EJ 336
CLR 4138
cd: preiser 90269/appian APR 5521/naxos 8.110858/symposium 1345

005/10-14 october 1928/electrola sessions in berlin singakademie

staatskapelle berlin/chor der staatsoper berlin/karl muck gotthelf pistor, tenor/cornelis bronsgeest, baritone/ ludwig hofmann, bass

wagner parsifal act three: prelude with concert ending and "heil mir dass ich dich wieder finde" to end of work

CLR 4609	EJ 373/D 1538/victor M 67
CLR 4610	
CLR 4598	EJ 374/D 1539/victor M 67
CLR 4599	
CLR 4600	EJ 375/D 1540/victor M 67
CLR 4601	
CLR 4602	EJ 376/D 1541/victor M 67
CLR 4603	
CLR 4604	EJ 377/D 1542/victor M 67
CLR 4605	
CLR 4612	EJ 378/D 1543/victor M 67
CLR 4613	
CLR 4614	EJ 379/D 1544/victor M 67
CLR 4615	
CLR 4616	EJ 380/D 1545/victor M 67
CLR 4617	

lp: preiser LV 100 (without prelude)/pearl OPAL 837-838
cd: pearl GEMMCDS 9843/naxos 8.110049-110050/ preiser 90270/hamburger archiv für gesangskunst/ centaur CRC 2142 (prelude only)

78rpm edition was also published in automatic coupling with the catalogue numbers D 7891-7898

006/21 november 1929/electrola session in berlin philharmonie

staatskapelle berlin/karl muck

wagner lohengrin: act three prelude
CLR 5806   unpublished
cd: appian APR 5521

wagner siegfried idyll
CLR 5807   EH 561/victor 7381
CLR 5808
CLR 5809   EH 562/victor 7382
CLR 5810
cd: pearl GEMMCDS 9843/symposium 1345/
naxos 8.110858

KARL MUCK: COMPOSER DISCOGRAPHY
session numbers enable cross-reference to the main chronological discography

LUDWIG VAN BEETHOVEN (1770-1827)
symphony no 7: first part of the fourth movement
001/camden new jersey 1917

HECTOR BERLIOZ (1803-1869)
la damnation de faust: marche hongroise and danse des sylphes
001/camden new jersey 1917

composer discography/continued

PIOTR TCHAIKOVSKY (1840-1893)
symphony no 4: fourth movement
001/camden new jersey 1917

orchestral suite no 1: marche miniature
001/camden new jersey 1917

casse noisette: valse des fleurs
001/camden new jersey 1917

RICHARD WAGNER (1813-1883)
der fliegende holländer overture
004/berlin 1928

götterdämmerung: siegfrieds rheinfahrt und trauermarsch
003/berlin 1927

composer discography/continued

wagner lohengrin: act three prelude
001/camden new jersey 1917
006/berlin 1929

die meistersinger von nürnberg overture
003/berlin 1927

parsifal act three
005/berlin 1928

parsifal prelude
003/berlin 1927

parsifal: verwandlungsmusik und gralsszane
002/bayreuth 1927

parsifal: blumenmädchenszene
002/bayreuth 1927

siegfried idyll
006/berlin 1929

composer discography/concluded
wagner tannhäuser overture
004/berlin 1928

tristan und isolde prelude
004/berlin 1928

ERMANNO WOLF-FERRARI (1876-1948)
il segreto di susanna overture
001/camden new jersey 1917

FRANZ VON HOESSLIN: CHRONOLOGICAL DISCOGRAPHY

001/august 1927/columbia sessions in bayreuth festspielhaus

orchester der bayreuther festspiele/franz von hoesslin
*ingeborg holmgren/maria nezadal/henriette gottlieb/
elli sendler/minny ruske-leopold/charlotte rückforth/
charlotte müller/maria peschken

wagner siegfried: act three prelude; siegfried durchschreitet das feuer
WAX 3000   L 2015/CLX 12523
WAX 3001
cd: preiser 90393/malibran CDRG 134

*wagner das rheingold: einzug der götter in walhall; gesang der rheintöchter
WAX 3002   L 2016/CLX 12524/GQX 10482/M 338
WAX 3003
cd: preiser 90393

*wagner die walküre: walkürenritt
WAX 3004   L 2017/CLX 12525/M 338
WAX 3005
cd: preiser 90393/malibran CDRG 134

001/august 1927/columbia sessions in bayreuth/concluded

wagner siegfried: waldweben
WAX 3009   L 2014/CLX 12522/M 337
cd: preiser 90393/malibran CDRG 134
the complete set of 1927 bayreuth recordings, also including items conducted by karl muck and siegfried wagner, was also published in the columbia international series

002/june 1929/pathe sessions in paris theatre des champs-elysees

orchestre et choeurs des concerts walter straram/
franz von hoesslin
henriette gottlieb/olga schramm-tschörner/
margarete klose/walter kirchhoff/ludwig weber/
ludwig hofmann/anny konetzni/emmy neiendorf/
frau glahes/olga forrai/maria peschken

wagner der ring des nibelungen, abridged version
das rheingold: lugt schwestern!; immer ist undank loges lohn
300 000   X 7196
300 000
cd: gebhardt JGCD 0016/cantus classics

002/june 1929/pathe sessions in paris/continued
das rheingold: über stock und stein; weiche wotan!
300 000   X 7197
300 348
lp: emi 1C181 30669-30678M (weiche wotan only)
cd: hamburger archiv für gesangskunst (weiche wotan only)/gebhardt JGCD 0016/cantus classics

das rheingold: einzug der götter in walhall;
die walküre: ein schwert verhiess mich der vater
300 000   X 7198
300 000
cd: gebhardt JGCD 0016/cantus classics

die walküre: winterstürme wichen dem
wonnemond; du bist der lenz
300 000   X 7199
300 000
cd: gebhardt JGCD 0016/cantus classics

die walküre: o süsseste wonne!...to end of act one
300 000   X 7200
300 000
cd: gebhardt JGCD 0016/cantus classics

die walküre: nun zäume dein ross!; hoiho toho!;
walkürenritt
300 339   X 7201
300 340
cd: gebhardt JGCD 0016/cantus classics

002/june 1929/pathe sessions in paris/continued

die walküre: wo ist brünnhild wo die verbrecherin?;
war es so schmählich?
300 000   X 7202
300 000
cd: gebhardt JGCD 0016/cantus classics

die walküre: leb wohl du kühnes herrliches kind!;
der augen leuchtendes paar
300 000   X 7203
300 000
cd: gebhardt JGCD 0016/cantus classics

die walküre: loge her!...to end of act three
300 000   X 7204
300 000
cd: gebhardt JGCD 0016/cantus classics

002/june 1929/pathe sessions in paris/continued
siegfried: nothung neidliches schwert!; dass der mein vater nicht ist
300 000   X 7205
300 000
cd: gebhardt JGCD 0016/cantus classics

siegfried: waldweben....to end of act two
300 000   X 7206
300 000
cd: gebhardt JGCD 0016/cantus classics

siegfried: kenntest du mich kühner spross; mit zerfochtener waffe (siegfried durchschreitet das feuer)
300 000   X 7207
300 000
cd: gebhardt JGCD 0016/cantus classics

siegfried: heil dir sonne!; ewig war ich
300 000   X 7208
300 000
cd: gebhardt JGCD 0016/cantus classics

siegfried: dich lieb ich so liebst du mich!... to end of act three
300 000   X 7209
300 000
cd: gebhardt JGCD 0016/cantus classics

002/june 1929/pathe sessions in paris/continued

götterdämmerung: siegfrieds rheinfahrt
300 000   X 7210
300 000
cd: gebhardt JGCD 0016/cantus classics

götterdämmerung: hier sitz ich zur wacht;
hoiho ihr gibichsmannen!
300 344   X 7211
300 342
cd: gebhardt JGCD 0016/cantus classics

götterdämmerung: gross glück und heil!;
frau sonne sendet lichte strahlen
300 343   X 7212
300 000
cd: gebhardt JGCD 0016/cantus classics

002/june 1929/pathe sessions in paris/concluded

götterdämmerung: ein albe führte mich hier
300 000   X 7213
300 000
cd: gebhardt JGCD 0016/cantus classics

götterdämmerung: brünnhilde heilige braut!;
siegfrieds trauermarsch
300 000   X 7214
300 000
cd: gebhardt JGCD 0016/cantus classics

götterdämmerung: starke scheite schichtet mir
dort....to end of act three
300 000   X 7215
300 000
cd: gebhardt JGCD 0016/cantus classics

FRANZ VON HOESSLIN: COMPOSER DISCOGRAPHY
items recorded in paris in 1929 constituted an abridged version of der ring des nibelungen

RICHARD WAGNER (1813-1883)
götterdämmerung: siegfrieds rheinfahrt; hier sitz ich zur wacht; hoiho ihr gibichsmannen!; gross glück und heil!; frau sonne sendet lichte strahlen; ein albe führte mich hier; brünnhild heilige braut!; siegfrieds trauermarsch; starke scheite schichtet mir dort!
002/paris 1929

das rheingold: immer ist undank loges lohn; über stock und stein; weiche wotan weiche!
002/paris 1929

das rheingold: einzug der götter in walhall
001/bayreuth 1927
002/paris 1929

composer discography/concluded

**wagner siegfried: nothung neidliches schwert!;
dass der mein vater nicht ist; act three prelude;
kenntest du mich kühner spross; heil dir sonne!;
ewig war ich; dich lieb ich wie du mich liebst**
002/paris 1929

**siegfried: waldweben; siegfried durchschreitet
das feuer**
001/bayreuth 1927
002/paris 1929

**die walküre: ein schwert verhiess mich der vater;
winterstürme wichen dem wonnemond; du bist
der lenz; o süsseste wonne!; nun zäume dein ross!;
wo ist brünnhild wo die verbrecherin?; war es so
schmählich?; leb wohl du kühnes herrliches kind;
der augen leuchtendes paar; loge her!**
002/paris 1929

die walküre: walkürenritt
001/bayreuth 1927
002/paris 1929

KARL ELMENDORFF: CHRONOLOGICAL DISCOGRAPHY

001/july 1928/columbia sessions without audience in bayreuth festspielhaus

orchester und männerchor der bayreuther festspiele/ karl elmendorff
nanny larsen-todsen/anny helm/gunnar graarud/ rudolf bockelmann/ivar andressen/joachim sattler/ hanns beer/gustav rödin

wagner tristan und isolde

act one
WAX 3934	L 2187/DWX 1273/M 101
WAX 3935	
WAX 3936	L 2188/DWX 1274/M 101
WAX 3937	
WAX 3938	L 2189/DWX 1275/M 101
WAX 3939	
WAX 3940	L 2190/DWX 1276/M 101
WAX 3941	
WAX 3942	L 2191/DWX 1277/M 101
WAX 3970	
WAX 3943	L 2192/DWX 1278/M 101
WAX 3944	
WAX 3945	L 2193/DWX 1279/M 101
WAX 3946	

001/july 1928/columbia sessions in bayreuth/continued
act two

WAX 4276	L 2194/DWX 1280/M 101
WAX 3971	
WAX 3972	L 2195/DWX 1281/M 101
WAX 3973	
WAX 3974	L 2196/DWX 1282/M 101
WAX 3975	
WAX 3976	L 2197/DWX 1283/M 101
WAX 3977	
WAX 3978	L 2198/DWX 1284/M 101
WAX 3979	
WAX 3980	L 2199/DWX 1285/M 101
WAX 3981	
WAX 3982	L 2200/DWX 1286/M 101
WAX 3947	
WAX 3948	L 2201/DWX 1287/M 101
WAX 3949	
WAX 3983	L 2202/DWX 1288/M 101
WAX 3984	

elmendorff

001/july 1928/columbia sessions in bayreuth/concluded
act three (heavily abridged)

WAX 4277	L 2203/DWX 1289/M 101
WAX 3950	
WAX 3951	L 2204/DWX 1290/M 101
WAX 3952	
WAX 3985	L 2205/DWX 1291/M 101
WAX 3953	
WAX 3986	L 2206/DWX 1292/M 101
WAX 3987	

lp: columbia (usa) EL 11/emi 1C181 03031-03033M
cd: malibran CDRG 102/grammofono AB 78295-78296/
arkadia 78052/preiser 90383/naxos 8.110200-110202/
cantus classics CACD 500 402

78rpm edition also issued in the columbia international series with the catalogue numbers LCX 64-83; WAX 4276 and WAX 4277 contained a spoken introduction by ernest newman on the motifs and their function (substituted for the french market by a version by messrs. schneider and berard with matrix numbers WLX 805 and WLX 806)

002/august 1930/columbia sessions without audience in bayreuth festspielhaus

orchester und chor der bayreuther festspiele/
karl elmendorff
sigismund pilinsky/maria müller/ruth jost-arden/
erna berger/herbert janssen/ivar andresen/geza
belti-pilinsky/joachim sattler/carl stralendorf/
georg von tschurtschenthaler

wagner tannhäuser

WAX 5684	LX 81/LWX 3300/LFX 112/M 151
WAX 5685	
WAX 5686	LX 82/LWX 3301/LFX 113/M 151
WAX 5687	
WAX 5688	LX 83/LWX 3302/LFX 114/M 151
WAX 5689	
WAX 5690	LX 84/LWX 3303/LFX 115/M 151
WAX 5691	
WAX 5692	LX 85/LWX 3304/LFX 116/M 151
WAX 5693	

002/august 1930/columbia sessions in bayreuth/continued

WAX 5694	LX 86/LWX 3305/LFX 117/M 151
WAX 5695	
WAX 5696	LX 87/LWX 3306/LFX 118/M 151
WAX 5697	
WAX 5698	LX 88/LWX 3307/LFX 119/M 151
WAX 5699	
WAX 5700	LX 89/LWX 3308/LFX 120/M 151
WAX 5701	
WAX 5702	LX 90/LWX 3309/LFX 121/M 151
WAX 5703	
WAX 5704	LX 91/LWX 3310/LFX 122/M 151
WAX 5705	
WAX 5706	LX 92/LWX 3311/LFX 123/M 151
WAX 5707	
WAX 5708	LX 93/LWX 3312/LFX 124/M 151
WAX 4899	
WAX 5710	LX 94/LWX 3313/LFX 125/M 151
WAX 5711	
WAX 5712	LX 95/LWX 3314/LFX 126/M 151
WAX 5713	
WAX 5714	LX 96/LWX 3315/LFX 127/M 151
WAX 5715	

002/august 1930/columbia sessions in bayreuth/concluded
WAX 5716   LX 97/LWX 3316/LFX 128/M 151
WAX 5717
WAX 5718   LX 98/LWX 3317/LFX 129/M 151
WAX 5719
lp: emi 1C137 03130-03132M
cd: pearl GEMMCD 9941/malibran CDRG 113/naxos 8.110094-110095/cantus classics CACD 500 286

78rpm edition also issued in the columbia international series with the catalogue numbers LCX 46-63; according to ward marston WAX 4899 was an earlier recording by ivar andressen (with another conductor) of the landgrave's address (ein furchtbares verbrechen ward hier begangen) which for unknown reasons was substituted for WAX 5709

003/july 1934/deutsche wochenschau film of rehearsal in bayreuth festspielhaus

orchester der bayreuther festspiele/karl elmendorff
frida leider/max lorenz

wagner götterdämmerung: zu neuen taten
concluding bars of the duet only
this extract (often misdated) can be seen in numerous film documentaries about wagner and bayreuth

004/4 august 1939/stage recording in bayreuth festspielhaus

orchester und chor der bayreuther festspiele/
karl elmendorff
maria müller/rudolf bockelmann/ludwig hofmann

wagner der fliegende holländer: mein kind du siehst mich auf der schwelle....to end of act two; steht euch nach frischem wein der sinn? (matrosenchor)
lp: unique opera records EJS 489

005/june 1942/electrola and reichsrundfunk sessions in dresden semperoper

sächsische staatskapelle dresden/karl elmendorff
margarete düren/josef hermann

mozart le nozze di figaro: se vuol ballare/sung in german
ORA 5515   unpublished
lp: preiser LV 167

mozart le nozze di figaro: crudel perche finora; cinque dieci!/sung in german
ORA 5516   DA 4502
ORA 5513
lp: acanta 72.221792 (cinque dieci only)/preiser LV 167

lortzing undine: es wohnt am seegestade
ORA 5517   unpublished
lp: preiser LV 167

elmendorff

006/21 july 1942/reichsrundfunk recording in bayreuth festspielhaus

orchester und chor der bayreuther festspiele/
karl elmendorff
marta fuchs/else fischer/camilla kallab/set svanholm/
egmont koch/friedrich dalberg/robert burg/hildegard jachnow/charlotte siewert/hilde scheppan/irmgard langhammer/margery booth

wagner götterdämmerung
cd: preiser 90164/music and arts CD 1058/omega opera archive OOA 1935/cantus classics CACD 500 892

007/2-3 march 1943/reichsrundfunk recordings in dresden semperoper

sächsische staatskapelle dresden/karl elmendorff
margarete teschemacher/elfriede trötschel/
lorenz fehenberger/karl wessely/sven nilsson/
heinrich pflanzl/mathieu ahlersmayer/robert burg

dvorak the jacobin, abridged version/sung in german
cd: profil medien PH 07031

wagner wesendonk-lieder: der engel; im treibhaus
(margarete teschemacher)
lp: acanta 22.226379

008/june 1943/electrola and reichsrundfunk sessions in dresden semperoper

sächsische staatskapelle dresden/chor der staatsoper dresden/karl elmendorff
margarete düren/willy treffner/heinrich tessmer/ josef hermann/kurt böhme

weber peter schmoll und seine nachbarn: gottes falke ist doch schön; puccini gianni schicchi: und der notar kommt
ORA 5988   unpublished
ORA 5994
lp: preiser LV 167
cd: preiser 89076 (weber only)

lortzing undine: was treibt euch an mich hieher zu verfolgen?; leoncavallo i pagliacci: so ben che difforme
2RA 5989   unpublished
2RA 5990
lp: preiser LV 167
cd: preiser 89076 (leoncavallo only)

008/june 1943/electrola and reichsrundfunk sessions in dresden/continued

verdi otello: roderigo beviam!; leoncavallo i pagliacci: si puo!/*sung in german*
2RA 6002   DB 7700
2RA 5991
lp: preiser LV 49
cd: preiser 89076/89545

wagner der fliegende holländer: durch sturm und bösen wind; beethoven fidelio: jetzt alter hat es eile!
2RA 5996   unpublished
2RA 5997
lp: preiser LV 167
cd: preiser 89968 (wagner only)/89076

wagner der fliegende holländer: wie hört ich recht?; die meistersinger von nürnberg: jerum jerum!
2RA 5998   unpublished
2RA 5999
lp: preiser LV 167
cd: preiser 89968 (holländer only)/89076

008/june 1943/electrola and reichsrundfunk sessions in dresden/concluded

lortzing zar und zimmermann: sonst spielt ich mit zepter; undine: nun ist's vollbracht
2RA 6001   unpublished
2RA 6003
lp: preiser LV 167 (zar und zimmermann only)

lortzing undine: schwanensang schwanenklang!
2RA 6004   unpublished

mozart cosi fan tutte: un aura amorosa; donizetti la favorita: una vergine/*sung in german*
unpublished
cd: preiser 89545

verdi messa da requiem: ingemisco; haydn die jahreszeiten: dem druck erlieget die natur
unpublished
cd: preiser 89545

009/23 june 1943/grammophon sessions in berlin

staatskapelle berlin/karl elmendorff

wagner die walküre: walkürenritt und feuerzauber
1496 ge IX   67642
1497 ge IX
lp: deutsche grammophon LPEM 19 393
cd: deutsche grammophon 479 1148

wagner götterdämmerung: siegfrieds rheinfahrt
1498 ge IX   67641
1499 ge IX
lp: deutsche grammophon LPEM 19 393/2721 113
cd: deutsche grammophon 479 1148

wagner siegfried: waldweben
1500 ge IX   67640
1501 ge IX
lp: deutsche grammophon LPEM 19 393

wagner das rheingold: einzug der götter in walhall
1502 ge IX   68430
lp: deutsche grammophon LPEM 19 393
cd: deutsche grammophon 479 1148

elmendorff

**010/22 november and 16-18 december 1943/
reichsrundfunk recording in dresden semperoper**

sächsische staatskapelle dresden/chor der staatsoper dresden/karl elmendorff
margarete teschemacher/elfriede trötschel/mathieu ahlersmayer/pavel mirov/sven nilsson/heinrich pflanzl/hans löbel/karl wessely/ina arowska/jakob felder/edith dietrich

goetz der widerspenstigen zähmung
cd: preiser 90416/cantus classics CACD 500 066
further recording session was held on 1 may 1944

011/1944/reichsrundfunk recording in dresden semperoper

sächsische staatskapelle dresden/chor der staatsoper dresden/karl elmendorff
maria cebotari/helena rott/elfriede trötschel/hans hopf/josef hermann/kurt böhme/georg hann

verdi luisa miller/*sung in german*
lp: preiser LM 11/acanta BB 21805
cd: preiser 90055/cantus classics CACD 500 019

012/1944/reichsrundfunk recordings in dresden semperoper

sächsische staatskapelle dresden/karl elmendorff
lorenz fehenberger/paul schöffler

mozart die entführung aus dem serail: o wie ängstlich!
cd: pilz CD 78008

mozart don giovanni: deh vieni alla finestra/*sung in german*
lp: acanta 22.226948

013/5 february 1944/deutsche wochenschau film in dresden semperoper

sächsische staatskapelle dresden/karl elmendorff
ballet der staatsoper dresden

von einem prinzessin turandot
film fragment only

014/1 june 1944/reichsrundfunk recording in dresden semperoper

sächsische staatskapelle dresden/chor der staatsoper dresden/karl elmendorff
margarete teschemacher/elfriede trötschel/lorenz fehenberger/kurt böhme/heinrich pflanzl/sven nilsson/arno schellenberg/karl wessely/charlotte krassel/edith dietrich

weber der freischütz
cd: preiser 90386/cantus classics 500 125/ audio encyclopaedia AE 209/profil medien PH 07060

015/20 june 1944/reichsrundfunk recording in dresden semperoper

sächsische staatskapelle dresden/chor der staatsoper dresden/karl elmendorff
mathieu ahlersmayer/kurt böhme/hans hopf/ marianne schech/margarete teschemacher/ elfriede weidlich/heinrich pflanzl/gottlob frick

mozart don giovanni/_sung in german_
lp: eterna 820 238-820 840/deutsche grammophon LPEM 19 250-19 252
cd: berlin classics 0325 001/cantus classics CACD 500 206/preiser 20023/audio encyclopaedia AE 208

016/3 august 1944/reichsrundfunk recordings in dresden semperoper

sächsische staatskapelle dresden/karl elmendorff

schubert symphony no 4 in c D417 "tragic"
lp: melodiya M10 46117 007
cd: tahra TAH 324-327

beethoven grosse fuge, arranged for strings
lp: melodiya M10 46117 007

elmendorff

017/21 september 1944/reichsrundfunk recordings in dresden semperoper

sächsische staatskapelle dresden/karl elmendorff
marianne schech/margarete teschemacher/max lorenz/kurt böhme/josef hermann

wagner tannhäuser: dich teure halle; allmächtige jungfrau/*schech*
lp: eterna 822 871 (dich teure halle)
cd: profil medien PH 07048

wagner die walküre: act one/*teschemacher/lorenz/böhme*
lp: preiser 0120 015-0120 016
cd: preiser 90015/tahra TAH 324-327/
profil medien PH 07048

wagner die walküre: wotans abschied und feuerzauber/*hermann*
lp: eterna 820 960/preiser 0120 015-0120 016/
acanta DE 23108-23109/40.23502
cd: tahra TAH 324-327/profil medien PH 07048/
hamburger archiv für gesangskunst

wagner götterdämmerung: blühenden lebens labende glut/*lorenz/hermann*
lp: acanta DE 23108-23109
cd: profil medien PH 07048

018/14-16 november 1944/reichsrundfunk recording in dresden steinsaal des hygienemuseums

sächsische staatskapelle dresden/chor der staatsoper dresden/karl elmendorff
marie-luise schilp/irma beilke/lorenz fehenberger/ hans hopf/arno schellenberg/gottlob frick/kurt böhme

auber fra diavolo/sung in german
lp: urania URLP 204/acanta 22.292691
cd: preiser 90349/cantus classics CACD 500 204/ audio encyclopaedia AE 208

019/28 november 1944/reichsrundfunk recording in dresden steinsaal des hygienemuseums

sächsische staatskapelle dresden/karl elmendorff

brahms symphony no 4 in e minor op 98
this unpublished recording may not survive in complete form

elmendorff

020/december 1944/reichsrundfunk recordings in dresden steinsaal des hygienemuseums

sächsische staatskapelle dresden/karl elmendorff
josef hermann

wagner siegfried: auf wolkigen höhen wohnen die götter
lp: acanta DE 23108-23109/40.23502
cd: hamburger archiv für gesangskunst/
profil medien PH 07048

weber euryanthe: kein schlaf gibt meinem wilden blute ruh'
lp: eterna 820 960/821 872/acanta DE 23108-23109
cd: berlin classics BC 20492/hamburger archiv für gesangskunst/preiser 90386

021/11 december 1944/grammophon and reichsrundfunk session in dresden steinsaal des hygienemuseums

sächsische staatskapelle dresden/karl elmendorff

von einem konzert für orchester

2880 ½ gs   68186
2881 ½ gs
2882 ½ gs   68187
2883 ½ gs
2884 ½ gs   68188
2885 ½ gs

subsequently issued on variable grade 78rpm discs with catalogue numbers 69488-69489

022/21-28 december 1944/reichsrundfunk recording in dresden steinsaal des hygienemuseums

sächsische staatskapelle dresden/chor der staatsoper dresden/karl elmendorff
marta fuchs/margarete teschemacher/karl erb/
helena rott/karl wessely/kurt böhme/georg hann/
gottlob frick

wolf der corregidor
lp: urania URLP 208/acanta 30.214087
cd: preiser 90182/cantus classics CACD 500 219/
audio encyclopaedia AE 209

023/1956/vox studio recording in stuttgart

orchester und chor der württembergischen staatsoper/
karl elmendorff

karl gester

wagner tannhäuser: act three prelude; wohl wusst ich hier sie im gebet zu finden; pilgerchor
45: vox VIP 45480

KARL ELMENDORFF: COMPOSER DISCOGRAPHY
session numbers enable cross reference to the main chronological discography

DANIEL AUBER (1782-1871)
fra diavolo
018/dresden 1944

LUDWIG VAN BEETHOVEN (1770-1827)
grosse fuge, arranged for strings
016/dresden 1944

fidelio: jetzt alter hat es eile!
008/dresden 1943

fidelio: gott welch dunkel hier!
012/dresden 1944

JOHANNES BRAHMS (1833-1897)
symphony no 4 in e minor op 98
019/dresden 1944

composer discography/continued

GAETONO DONIZETTI (1797-1848)
la favorita: una vergine
008/dresden 1943

ANTONIN DVORAK (1841-1904)
the jakobin
007/dresden 1943

GOTTFRIED VON EINEM (1918-1996)
konzert für orchester
021/dresden 1944

prinzessin turandot
013/dresden 1944

HERMANN GOETZ (1840-1876)
der widerspenstigen zähmung
010/dresden 1943

FRANZ JOSEF HAYDN (1732-1809)
die jahreszeiten: dem druck erlieget die natur
008/dresden 1943

composer discography/continued
RUGGIERO LEONCAVALLO (1858-1919)
i pagliacci: si puo!; so ben che difforme
008/dresden 1943

ALBERT LORTZING (1801-1851)
undine: es wohnt am seegestade
005/dresden 1942

undine: was treibt euch an mich hieher zu verfolgen?;
nun ist's vollbracht; schwanensang schwanenklang!
008/dresden 1943

zar und zimmermann: sonst spielt' ich mit zepter
008/dresden 1943

WOLFGANG AMADEUS MOZART (1756-1791)
cosi fan tutte: un aura amorosa
008/dresden 1943

don giovanni
015/dresden 1944

composer discography/continued

mozart don giovanni: deh vieni alla finestra
012/dresden 1944

mozart die entführung aus dem serial: o wie ängstlich!
012/dresden 1944

mozart le nozze di figaro: se vuol ballare; crudel perche finora?
005/dresden 1942

GIACOMO PUCCINI (1858-1924)
gianni schicchi: und der notar kommt
008/dresden 1943

FRANZ SCHUBERT (1797-1828)
symphony no 4 in c D417 "tragic"
016/dresden 1944

composer discography/continued

GIUSEPPE VERDI (1813-1901)
luisa miller
011/dresden 1944

otello: roderigo beviam!
008/dresden 1943

messa da requiem: ingemisco
008/dresden 1943

RICHARD WAGNER (1813-1883)
der fliegende holländer: mein kind du siehst mich auf der schwelle; steht euch nach frischem wein der sinn?
004/bayreuth 1939

der fliegende holländer: durch sturm und bösen wind; wie hört' ich recht?
008/dresden 1943

götterdämmerung
006/bayreuth 1942

götterdämmerung: zu neuen taten
003/bayreuth 1934

composer discography/continued

wagner götterdämmerung: siegfrieds rheinfahrt
009/berlin 1943

götterdämmerung: blühenden lebens labende glut
017/dresden 1944

die meistersinger von nürnberg: jerum jerum!
008/dresden 1943

das rheingold: einzug der götter in walhall
009/berlin 1943

siegfried: waldweben
009/berlin 1943

siegfried: auf wolkigen höhen wohnen die götter
020/dresden 1944

tannhäuser
002/bayreuth 1930

composer discography/continued

wagner tannhäuser: act three prelude
023/stuttgart 1956

tannhäuser: dich teure halle; allmächtige jungfrau
017/dresden 1944

tannhäuser: wohl wusst' ich hier sie im gebet zu finden; pilgerchor
023/stuttgart 1956

tristan und isolde
001/bayreuth 1928

die walküre: act one
017/dresden 1944

die walküre: walkürenritt und feuerzauber
009/berlin 1943

die walküre: wotans abschied und feuerzauber
017/dresden 1944

wesendonk-lieder: der engel; im treibhaus
007/dresden 1943

composer discography/concluded

CARL MARIA VON WEBER (1786-1826)
euryanthe: kein schlaf gibt meinem wilden blute ruh'
020/dresden 1944

der freischütz
014/dresden 1944

peter schmoll und seine nachbarn: gottes falke ist doch schön
008/dresden 1943

HUGO WOLF (1860-1903)
der corregidor
022/dresden 1944

Books published by Travis & Emery Music Bookshop:
Anon.: Hymnarium Sarisburiense, cum Rubricis et Notis Musicis.
Anon.: Säcularfeier des Geburtstages von Ludwig van Beethoven
Agricola, Johann Friedrich from Tosi: Anleitung zur Singkunst.
Allen, Percy: The Stage Life of Mrs. Stirling: With ... C19th Theatre
Bach, C.P.E.: edited W. Emery: Nekrolog or Obituary Notice of J.S. Bach.
Bateson, Naomi Judith: Alcock of Salisbury
Bathe, William: A Briefe Introduction to the Skill of Song
Berlioz, Hector: Autobiography of Hector Berlioz, (2 vols.)
Buckley, Robert John: Sir Edward Elgar
Burney, Charles: The Present State of Music in France and Italy
Burney, Charles: The Present State of Music in Germany, The Netherlands ...
Burney, Charles: Account of an Infant Musician
Burney, Charles: An Account of the Musical Performances ... Handel
Burney, Karl: Nachricht von Georg Friedrich Handel's Lebensumstanden.
Burns, Robert: The Caledonian Musical Museum .. Best Scotch Songs. (1810)
Cobbett, W.W.: Cobbett's Cyclopedic Survey of Chamber Music. (2 vols.)
Corrette, Michel: Le Maitre de Clavecin
Cox, John Edmund: Musical Recollections of the Last Half Century. (2 vols.)
Crimp, Bryan: Dear Mr. Rosenthal ... Dear Mr. Gaisberg ...
Crimp, Bryan: Solo: The Biography of Solomon
Crotch, William: Substance of Several Courses of Lectures on Music
d'Indy, Vincent: Beethoven: Biographie Critique
d'Indy, Vincent: Beethoven: A Critical Biography
d'Indy, Vincent: Cesar Franck (in English)
d'Indy, Vincent: César Franck (in French)
Dianna, B.A.: Benjamin Britten's Holy Theatre
Dolge, Alfred: Pianos and Their Makers. A Comprehensive History
Fischhof, Joseph: Versuch einer Geschichte des Clavierbaues. (Faksimile 1853).
Fuller-Maitland, J.A.: The Music of Parry and Stanford
Geminiani, Francesco: The Art of Playing the Violin.
Häuser: Musikalisches Lexikon. 2 vols in one.
Hawkins, John: A General History of the Science & Practice of Music (5 vols.)
Holmes, Edward: A Ramble among the Musicians of Germany
Hopkins, Antony: The Concertgoer's Companion - Bach to Haydn.
Hopkins, Antony: The Concertgoer's Companion – Holst to Webern.
Hopkins, Antony: Music All Around Me
Hopkins, Antony: Sounds of Music / Sounds of the Orchestra
Hopkins, Antony: The Nine Symphonies of Beethoven
Hopkins, Antony: Understanding Music

Books published by Travis & Emery Music Bookshop:

Hopkins, Edward & Rimboult, Edward: The Organ. Its History & Construction.
Hunt, John: - see separate list of discographies at the end of these titles
Iliffe, Frederick: The Forty-Eight Preludes and Fugues of John Sebastian Bach
Isaacs, Lewis: Hänsel and Gretel. A Guide to Humperdinck's Opera.
Isaacs, Lewis: Königskinder (Royal Children). Guide to Humperdinck's Opera.
Kastner: Manuel Général de Musique Militaire
Kenney, Charles Lamb: A Memoir of Michael William Balfe
Klein, Hermann: Thirty years of musical Life in London, 1870-1900
Lacassagne, M. l'Abbé Joseph : Traité Général des élémens du Chant
Lascelles (née Catley), Anne: The Life of Miss Anne Catley.
McCormack, John: John McCormack: His Own Life Story.
Mainwaring, John: Memoirs of the Life of the Late George Frederic Handel
Malcolm, Alexander: A Treaty of Music: Speculative, Practical and Historical
Manshardt, Thomas: Aspects of Cortot
Marx, Adolph Bernhard: Die Kunst des Gesanges, Theoretisch-Practisch
May, Florence: The Life of Brahms
May, Florence: The Girlhood Of Clara Schumann: Clara Wieck And Her Time.
Mellers, Wilfrid: Angels of the Night: Popular Female Singers of Our Time
Mellers, Wilfrid: Bach and the Dance of God
Mellers, Wilfrid: Beethoven and the Voice of God
Mellers, Wilfrid: Caliban Reborn - Renewal in Twentieth Century Music
Mellers, Wilfrid: Darker Shade of Pale, A Backdrop to Bob Dylan
Mellers, Wilfrid: François Couperin and the French Classical Tradition
Mellers, Wilfrid: Harmonious Meeting
Mellers, Wilfrid: Le Jardin Retrouvé, The Music of Frederic Mompou
Mellers, Wilfrid: Music and Society, England and the European Tradition
Mellers, Wilfrid: Music in a New Found Land: … … American Music
Mellers, Wilfrid: Romanticism and the Twentieth Century (from 1800)
Mellers, Wilfrid: The Masks of Orpheus: …… the Story of European Music.
Mellers, Wilfrid: The Sonata Principle (from c. 1750)
Mellers, Wilfrid: Vaughan Williams and the Vision of Albion
Newmarch, Rosa: Henry J. Wood
Newmarch, Rosa: Jean Sibelius
Newmarch, Rosa: Mary Wakefield, a Memoir
Newmarch, Rosa: The Concert-Goer's Library
Newmarch, Rosa: The Music of Czechoslovakia
Newmarch, Rosa: The Russian Opera.
Nicholas, Jeremy: Godowsky, the Pianists' Pianist
Niecks, Frederick: The Life oc Chopin. (2 vols.)

Books published by Travis & Emery Music Bookshop:

Panchianio, Cattuffio: Rutzvanscad Il Giovine
Pearce, Charles: Sims Reeves, Fifty Years of Music in England.
Pepusch, John Christopher: A Treatise on Harmony ...
Pettitt, Stephen: Philharmonia Orchestra: A Record of Achievement, 1948-1985
Pettitt, Stephen (ed. Hunt): Philharmonia Orchestra: Discography 1945-1987
Playford, John: An Introduction to the Skill of Musick.
Porte, John: Sir Charles Villiers Stanford.
Quantz, Johann: Versuch einer Anweisung die Flöte traversiere zu spielen.
Rameau, Jean-Philippe: Code de Musique Pratique, ou Methodes.
Rameau, Jean-Philippe: Erreurs sur La Musique dans l'Encyclopédie
Rastall, Richard: The Notation of Western Music.
Rimbault, Edward: The Pianoforte, Its Origins, Progress, and Construction.
Rousseau, Jean Jacques: Dictionnaire de Musique
Rubinstein, Anton : Guide to the proper use of the Pianoforte Pedals.
Sainsbury, John S.: Dictionary of Musicians. (1825). (2 vols.)
Schumann, Clara & Brahms, Johannes: Letters 1853-1896. (2 vols.)
Scott-Sutherland: Arnold Bax
Serré de Rieux, Jean de : Les dons des Enfans de Latone
Simpson, Christopher: A Compendium of Practical Musick in Five Parts
Smyth, Ethel: Impressions That Remained. (2 vols.)
Spohr, Louis: Autobiography
Spohr, Louis: Grand Violin School
Tans'ur, William: A New Musical Grammar; or The Harmonical Spectator
Terry, Charles Sanford: Bach's Chorals – Parts 1, 2 and 3.
Terry, Charles Sanford: John Christian Bach
Terry, Charles Sanford: J.S. Bach's Original Hymn-Tunes - Congregational Use.
Terry, Charles Sanford: Four-Part Chorals of J.S. Bach. (German & English)
Terry, Charles Sanford: Joh. Seb. Bach, Cantata Texts, Sacred and Secular.
Terry, Charles Sanford: The Origins of the Family of Bach Musicians.
Tosi, Pierfrancesco: Opinioni de' Cantori Antichi, e Moderni
Tosi, Pierfrancesco: Observations on the Florid Song.
Tovey, Donald Francis: A Musician Talks, The Integrity of Music
Tovey, Donald Francis: A Musician Talks, Musical Textures
Tovey, Donald Francis: A Companion to "The Art of the Fugue" J.S. Bach
Tovey, Donald Francis: A Companion to Beethoven's Pianoforte Sonatas
Tovey, Donald Francis: Beethoven
Tovey, Donald Francis: Essays in Musical Analysis. (6 vols.).
Tovey, Donald Francis: The integrity of music
Tovey, Donald Francis: Musical Textures

Books published by Travis & Emery Music Bookshop:

Tovey, Donald Francis: Some English Symphonists
Tovey, Donald Francis: The Main Stream of Music.
Van der Straeten, Edmund: History of the Violoncello, The Viol da Gamba …
Van der Straeten, Edmund: History of the Violin, Its Ancestors… (2 vols.)
Walther, J. G. [Waltern]: Musicalisches Lexikon [Musikalisches Lexicon]
Wagner, Richard: Beethoven (Leipzig 1870)
Wagner, Richard: Lebens-Bericht (Leipzig 1884)
Wagner, Richard: The Musaic of the Future (Translated by E. Dannreuther).
Wyndham, Henry Saxe: The Annals of Covent Garden Theatre. (2 vols.)
Zwirn, Gerald: Stranded Stories From The Operas

Music published by Travis & Emery Music Bookshop:

Bach, Johann Sebastian: Sacred Songs for SCTB, arranged by Franz Wullner.
Bax, Arnold: Symphony #5, Arranged for Piano Four Hands by Walter Emery
Beranger, Pierre Jean de: Musique Des Chansons de Beranger: Airs Notes ...
Bizet, Georges: Djamileh. Vocal Score.
Donizetti, Gaetano: Betly. Dramma Giocoso in Due Atti. Vocal Score.
Frescobaldi, Girolamo: D'Arie Musicali per Cantarsi. Primo & Secondo Libro.
Handel, Purcell, Boyce, Greene ... Calliope or English Harmony: Volume First.
Hopkins, Antony: Sonatine
Purcell, Henry et al: Harmonia Sacra … The First Book, (1726)
Purcell, Henry et al: Harmonia Sacra … Book II (1726)
Sullivan, Arthur Seymour: Ivanhoe. Vocal score.
Sullivan, Arthur Seymour: The Rose of Persia. Vocal Score.
Weckerlin, Jean-Baptiste: Chansons Populaires du Pays de France

Other Books, not on Music:

Anon: A Collection of Testimonies Concerning Several Ministers of the Gospel Amongst People called Quakers, Deceased. [Facsimile of 1760 edn.].
Sandeman-Allen, Arthur: Bee-keeping with Twenty hives.

Available from: Travis & Emery at 17 Cecil Court, London, UK.
(+44) (0) 20 7 240 2129. email on sales@travis-and-emery.com .

Discographies by John Hunt.

3 Italian Conductors and 7 Viennese Sopranos: 10 Discographies: Arturo Toscanini, Guido Cantelli, Carlo Maria Giulini, Elisabeth Schwarzkopf, Irmgard Seefried, Elisabeth Gruemmer, Sena Jurinac, Hilde Gueden, Lisa Della Casa, Rita Streich.

A Gallic Trio: 3 Discographies: Charles Muench, Paul Paray, Pierre Monteux.

A Notable Quartet: 4 Discographies: Gundula Janowitz, Christa Ludwig, Nicolai Gedda, Dietrich Fischer-Dieskau.

American Classics: The Discographies of Leonard Bernstein & Eugene Ormand

Antal Dorati 1906-1988: Discography and Concert Register.

Austro-Hungarian Pianists, Discographies of Lili Kraus, Friedrich Gulda, Ingrid Haebler

Back From The Shadows: 4 Discographies: Willem Mengelberg, Dimitri Mitropoulos, Hermann Abendroth, Eduard Van Beinum.

Carlo Maria Giulini: Discography and Concert Register.

Columbia 33CX Label Discography.

Concert Hall Discography: Concert Hall Society and Concert Hall Record Club

Conductors On The Yellow Label: 8 Discographies: Fritz Lehmann, Ferdinand Leitner, Ferenc Fricsay, Eugen Jochum, Leopold Ludwig, Artur Rother, Franz Konwitschny, Igor Markevitch.

Dirigenten der DDR: Conductors of the German Democratic Republic

From Adam to Webern: the Recordings of von Karajan.

Frosh: Discography of the Richard Strauss Opera Die Frau ohne Schatten

Giants of the Keyboard: 6 Discographies: Wilhelm Kempff, Walter Gieseking, Edwin Fischer, Clara Haskil, Wilhelm Backhaus, Artur Schnabel.

Gramophone Stalwarts: 3 Separate Discographies: Bruno Walter, Erich Leinsdorf, Georg Solti.

Great Violinists: 3 Discographies: David Oistrakh, Wolfgang Schneiderhan, Arthur Grumiaux.

Hans Knappertsbusch: Kna: Concert Register and Discography of Hans Knappertsbusch, 1888-1965. Second Edition.

Her Master's Voice: Concert Register and Discography of Dame Elisabeth Schwarzkopf [Third Edition].

Hungarians in Exile: 3 Discographies: Fritz Reiner, Antal Dorati, George Szell.

Leopold Stokowski (1882-1977): Discography and Concert Register

Leopold Stokowski: Discography and Concert Listing.

Leopold Stokowski: Second Edition of the Discography.

Makers of the Philharmonia: 11 Discographies Alceo Galliera, Walter Susskind, Paul Kletzki, Nicolai Malko, Issay Dobrowen, Lovro Von Matacic, Efrem Kurtz, Otto Ackermann, Anatole Fistoulari, George Weldon, Robert Irving.

Metropolitan Sopranos: 4 Discographies: Rosa Ponselle, Eleanor Steber, Zinka Milanov, Leontyne Price.

Mezzo and Contraltos: 5 Discographies: Janet Baker, Margarete Klose, Kathleen Ferrier, Giulietta Simionato, Elisabeth Hoengen.

Mid-Century Conductors and More Viennese Singers: 10 Discographies: Karl Boehm, Victor De Sabata, Hans Knappertsbusch, Tullio Serafin, Clemens Krauss, Anton Dermota, Leonie Rysanek, Eberhard Waechter, Maria Reining, Erich Kunz.

More 20th Century Conductors: 7 Discographies: Eugen Jochum, Ferenc Fricsay, Carl Schuricht, Felix Weingartner, Josef Krips, Otto Klemperer, Erich Kleiber.
More Giants of the Keyboard: 5 Discographies: Claudio Arrau, Gyorgy Cziffra, Vladimir Horowitz, Dinu Lipatti, Artur Rubinstein.
More Musical Knights: 4 Discographies: Hamilton Harty, Charles Mackerras, Simon Rattle, John Pritchard.
Musical Knights: 6 Discographies: Henry Wood, Thomas Beecham, Adrian Boult, John Barbirolli, Reginald Goodall, Malcolm Sargent.
Philharmonic Autocrat 1: Discography of: Herbert Von Karajan [3rd Edition]
Philharmonic Autocrat 2: Concert Register of Herbert Von Karajan 2nd. Ed.
Philharmonic Autocrat: Discography of Herbert von Karajan (1908-1989). 4th Ed..
Philips Minigroove: Second Extended Version of the European Discography.
Pianists For The Connoisseur: 6 Discographies: Arturo Benedetti Michelangeli, Alfred Cortot, Alexis Weissenberg, Clifford Curzon, Solomon, Elly Ney.
Record Pioneers: Richard Strauss, Hans Pfitzner, Oskar Fried, Oswald Kabasta, Karl Muck, Franz Von Hoesslin, Karl Elmendorff.
Sächsische Staatskapelle Dresden: Complete Discography.
Singers of the Third Reich: 5 Discographies: Helge Roswaenge, Tiana Lemnitz, Franz Voelker, Maria Mueller, Max Lorenz.
Singers on the Yellow Label: 7 Discographies: Maria Stader, Elfriede Troetschel, Annelies Kupper, Wolfgang Windgassen, Ernst Haefliger, Josef Greindl, Kim Borg
Six Wagnerian Sopranos: 6 Discographies: Frieda Leider, Kirsten Flagstad, Astrid Varnay, Martha Moedl, Birgit Nilsson, Gwyneth Jones.
Staatskapelle Berlin. The shellac era 1916-1962.
Sviatoslav Richter: Pianist of the Century: Discography.
Teachers and Pupils: 7 Discographies: Elisabeth Schwarzkopf, Maria Ivoguen, Maria Cebotari, Meta Seinemeyer, Ljuba Welitsch, Rita Streich, Erna Berger
Tenors in a Lyric Tradition: 3 Discographies: Peter Anders, Walther Ludwig, Fritz Wunderlich.
The Art of the Diva: 3 Discographies: Claudia Muzio, Maria Callas, Magda Olivero.
The Furtwaengler Sound Sixth Edition: Discography and Concert Listing.
The Furtwängler Sound. Discography of Wilhelm Furtwängler. Seventh Edition.
The Great Dictators: 3 Discographies: Evgeny Mravinsky, Artur Rodzinski, Sergiu Celibidache.
The Lyric Baritone: 5 Discographies: Hans Reinmar, Gerhard Huesch, Josef Metternich, Hermann Uhde, Eberhard Waechter.
The Post-War German Tradition: 5 Discographies: Rudolf Kempe, Joseph Keilberth, Wolfgang Sawallisch, Rafael Kubelik, Andre Cluytens.
Wagner Im Festspielhaus: Discography of the Bayreuth Festival.
Wiener Philharmoniker 1 - Vienna Philharmonic and Vienna State Opera Orchestras: Discography Part 1 1905-1954.
Wiener Philharmoniker 2 - Vienna Philharmonic and Vienna State Opera Orchestras: Discography Part 2 1954-1989.
Wiener Staatsoper: 348 complete relays

Available from: Travis & Emery at 17 Cecil Court, London, UK.
(+44) (0) 20 7 240 2129. email on sales@travis-and-emery.com .

www.ingramcontent.com/pod-product-compliance
Lightning Source LLC
Chambersburg PA
CBHW070824250426
43671CB00036B/2066